This book belongs to:

T0282033

_____

Table of Contents

Table of Contents

I Can Checklist:
Number Sense

Read, represent, compose, and decompose whole numbers up to and including 200, using a variety of tools and strategies, and describe various ways they are used in everyday life. For example,

- *I can read the number 178 and break it down into 100, 70, and 8.*
- *I can use counting blocks to represent the number 145, using one block of 100, four blocks of 10, and five blocks of 1.*
- *I can explain that when I am counting my pencils, I am using numbers in my everyday life.*

Compare and order whole numbers up to and including 200, in various contexts. For example,

- *I can line up the numbers 32, 178, 109, and 67 in order from smallest to largest.*
- *I can explain that 120 is greater than 105.*
- *I can put the numbers of pages in my three favourite books in order from least to greatest.*

Estimate the number of objects in collections of up to 200 and verify their estimates by counting. For example,

- *I can look at a jar of jelly beans and estimate that there are about 150 inside, then count them to check my guess.*
- *I can estimate that there are around 100 leaves on a branch of a tree and then count them to check if my estimate is correct.*

Count to 200, including by 20s, 25s, and 50s, using a variety of tools and strategies. For example,

- *I can count to 200 by ones, starting from one.*
- *I can count to 200 by 20s, saying "20, 40, 60, 80..." until I reach 200.*
- *I can count to 200 by 50s, saying "50, 100, 150, 200."*

Describe what makes a number even or odd. For example,

- *I can explain that a number is even or odd if I can divide it into equal groups and there are or aren't any remainders.*
- *I can identify that numbers such as 2, 4, 6, 8, and 10 are even, while numbers such as 1, 3, 5, 7, and 9 are odd.*

Math Is Everywhere!

Find pictures that show how we use numbers.
Cut them out and stick them below to make a collage.

Representing Numbers in Different Ways

There are different ways to write a number.

127   **1 hundred 2 tens 7 ones**

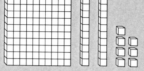

100 + 20 + 7

Circle two correct ways to make each number.

1

155

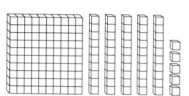

50 + 5

1 hundred +
5 tens + 5 ones

2

132

100 + 30 + 2

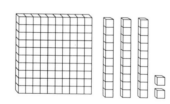

3 tens + 2 ones

3

27

2 tens + 9 ones

20 + 7

4

90

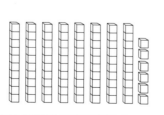

9 tens + 0 ones

80 + 10

I can represent Numbers in different ways.

Counting Tens and Ones

Count the tens and the ones. Write how many blocks in all.

1 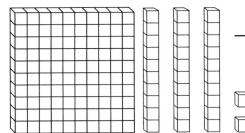 _____ hundreds _____ tens _____ ones

_____ + _____ + _____

There are _____ blocks.

2 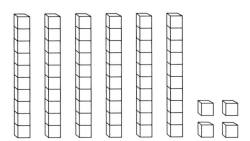 _____ tens _____ ones

_____ + _____

There are _____ blocks.

3 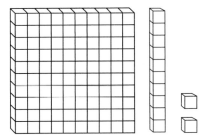 _____ hundreds _____ tens _____ ones

_____ + _____ + _____

There are _____ blocks.

4 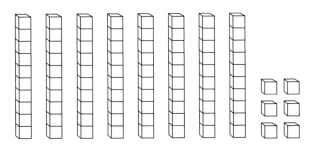 _____ tens _____ ones

_____ + _____

There are _____ blocks.

Writing Numbers in Written Form

1 one	2 two	3 three	4 four	5 five	6 six	7 seven
8 eight	9 nine	10 ten	11 eleven	12 twelve	13 thirteen	14 fourteen
15 fifteen	16 sixteen	17 seventeen	18 eighteen	19 nineteen	20 twenty	30 thirty
40 forty	50 fifty	60 sixty	70 seventy	80 eighty	90 ninety	100 hundred

1 Write the number in **written form**.

a 70 _____

b 15 _____

c 183 _____

d 120 _____

2 Point Amour Lighthouse is 33 m tall. Write the height in **written form**.

_____

3 The distance between Toronto, ON, and London, ON, is 194 km. Write the distance in **written form**.

_____

I can write numbers in written form.

Writing Numbers in Different Ways

175 is a **three-digit** number written in **Standard Form**.

The **digit 1** stands for **100**.

The **digit 7** stands for **70**.

The **digit 5** stands for **5**.

Place Value Chart

hundreds	tens	ones
1	7	5

Express **175** different ways:

- **Expanded Form:** 100 + 70 + 5
- **Written Form:** one hundred seventy-five

1 Write the numbers in expanded form.

a 96 _____

b 164 _____

c 113 _____

d 152 _____

2 Write the numbers in standard form.

a 100 + 30 + 8 _____

b 100 + 10 + 6 _____

c 100 + 70 + 9 _____

d 100 + 20 + 4 _____

3 Circle the value of the underlined digit.

a 1<u>4</u>3   4 tens   4 ones

b <u>1</u>82   1 ten   1 hundred

c 17<u>6</u>   6 ones   6 hundreds

d 1<u>5</u>0   5 tens   5 ones

Skip Counting

1 Count forward by 5s. Fill in the missing numbers.

20					

2 Count forward by 20s. Fill in the missing numbers.

50			

3 Count forward by 10s. Fill in the missing numbers.

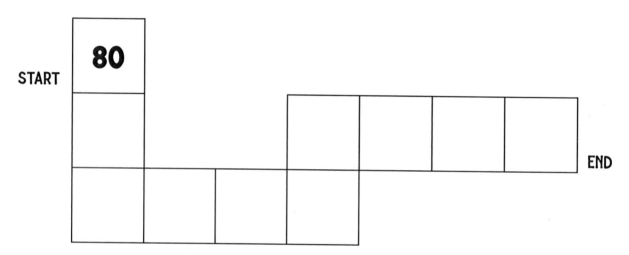

4 Count forward by 20s. Fill in the missing numbers.

I can skip count.

Counting Practice

1 Count forward by 10s. Fill in the missing numbers.

150					

2 Count forward by 25s. Fill in the missing numbers.

25					

3 Count forward by 2s. Fill in the missing numbers.

156					

4 Count backward by 1s. Fill in the missing numbers.

182					

5 Count backward by 10s. Fill in the missing numbers.

100					

6 Count backward by 2s. Fill in the missing numbers.

120					

Comparing Numbers

Fill in the blank with the correct symbol to compare.

greater than   less than   equal to

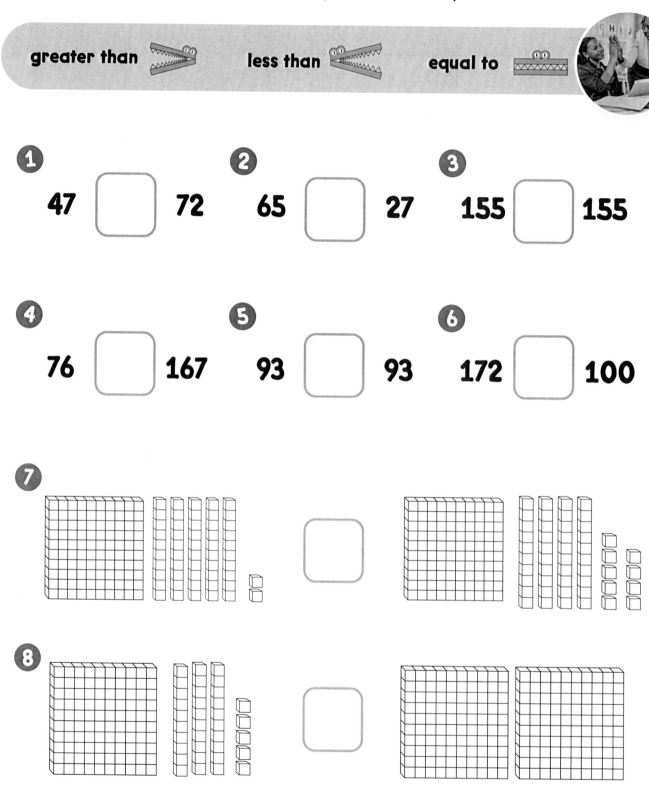

1 47 ☐ 72

2 65 ☐ 27

3 155 ☐ 155

4 76 ☐ 167

5 93 ☐ 93

6 172 ☐ 100

7

8

I can compare numbers.

Ordering Numbers

Numbers can be ordered from least to greatest, or from greatest to least.

least to greatest	greatest to least
72, 77, 83	**83, 77, 72**

1 Circle the greatest number in each pair.

ⓐ 78 or 87   ⓑ 165 or 132   ⓒ 52 or 15   ⓓ 98 or 198

2 Circle the smallest number in each pair.

ⓐ 150 or 50   ⓑ 100 or 110   ⓒ 37 or 17   ⓓ 200 or 20

3 Order the numbers from least to greatest.

ⓐ 72, 99, 25, 55   _____, _____, _____, _____

ⓑ 200, 120, 48, 190   _____, _____, _____, _____

4 Order the numbers from greatest to least.

ⓐ 46, 96, 13, 77   _____, _____, _____, _____

ⓑ 125, 102, 179, 188   _____, _____, _____, _____

5 Mr. Chang bought 33 onions, 41 carrots, 17 potatoes, and 24 olives. Sort the amounts from greatest to least.

_____, _____, _____, _____

Identifying Odd and Even Numbers

Look at the ones digits to see if a number is odd or even.
Odd numbers end in 1, 3, 5, 7, or 9.
Even numbers end in 0, 2, 4, 6, or 8.

Colour the odd numbers **blue**.
Colour the even numbers **red**.

87   25   46   71   88   99   16   61   62   100   39   58   46   70   33   29   115   54   199   2   97   200   14   93   10   6

  ✓ **I can identify odd odd even numbers.**

Estimating and Counting

Estimation is a smart guess. It is like thinking, "about how many?" without counting all the way.

Estimate, then count the total number of objects in each set.

1

Estimate: _____

Actual number: _____

2

Estimate: _____

Actual number: _____

3

Estimate: _____

Actual number: _____

Composing Numbers

To **compose a number**, take the hundreds, tens, and ones and add them together to make the whole number.

hundreds	tens	ones
100	70	3

173

Compose the numbers.

1 100 60 3

2 20 8

3 50 2

4 100 90 5

5 100 10 6

6 70 9

I can compose numbers.

Decomposing Numbers

To **decompose a number**, take it apart to make hundreds, tens, and ones. Its parts can be added together to make the whole.

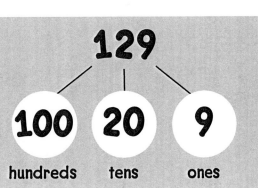

129
100 20 9
hundreds   tens   ones

Decompose the numbers.

1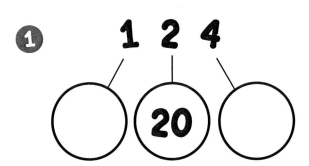

1 2 4
20

2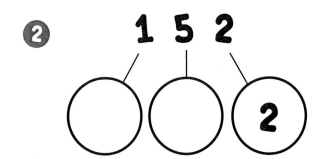

1 5 2
2

3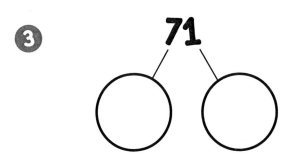

71

4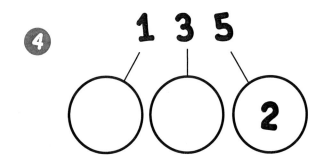

1 3 5
2

5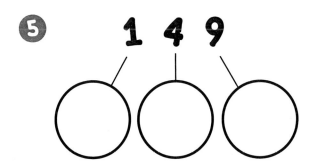

1 4 9

6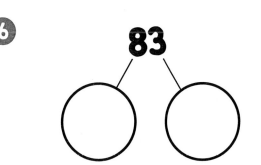

83

Show What You Know!

1 Write the number 145 in two different ways.

    a Written Form: _____

    b Expanded Form: _____

2 Count forward by 5s. Fill in the missing numbers.

105					

3 Fill in the blank with >, <, or = to compare.

    a   **b**   **c**

   187 [ ] 199   54 [ ] 54   23 [ ] 13

4 Order the numbers from least to greatest.

   167, 125, 180, 89   _____, _____, _____, _____

5 Order the numbers from greatest to least.

   101, 110, 200, 100   _____, _____, _____, _____

6 Circle the value of the underlined digit.

    a   1<u>9</u>2   9 tens   9 ones   **b**   <u>1</u>65   1 ten   1 hundred

Show What You Know! (continued)

7 Circle whether the number below is **EVEN** or **ODD**.

104 :   EVEN   ODD

8 Circle two correct ways to make each number.

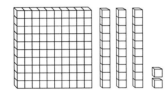 132   100 + 30 + 2   1 hundred + 30 ones

9 Estimate, then count the total number of objects in the set.

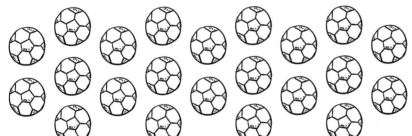

Estimate: _____

Actual number: _____

10 Compose or decompose the numbers.

a   90   4

b   1 6 5

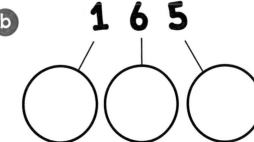

I Can Checklist:
Fractions

Use drawings to represent, solve, and compare the results of fair-share problems that involve sharing up to 10 items among 2, 3, 4, and 6 sharers, including problems that result in whole numbers, mixed numbers, and fractional amounts. For example,

- *I can* draw a picture of 10 apples and divide them evenly among 2 baskets, and explain that each basket gets 5 apples.

- *I can* draw 9 candies and share them equally among 3 friends, and explain that each friend gets 3 candies.

- *I can* draw 8 cookies and divide them into 4 groups, and explain that each group contains 2 cookies.

Recognize that one third and two sixths of the same whole are equal, in fair-sharing contexts. For example,

- *I can* cut a pizza into 3 equal parts and explain that taking one part is the same as having one third of the pizza.

- *I can* cut the same pizza into 6 parts and explain that taking two parts is the same as having two sixths of the pizza, which is the same as one third.

- *I can* draw a circle, divide it into 3 equal parts, colour one part, then divide the same circle into 6 equal parts and colour two parts to show that one third is equal to two sixths.

Equal and Not Equal Parts

Colour the shapes that show equal parts (blue).

Colour the shapes that do not show equal parts (red).

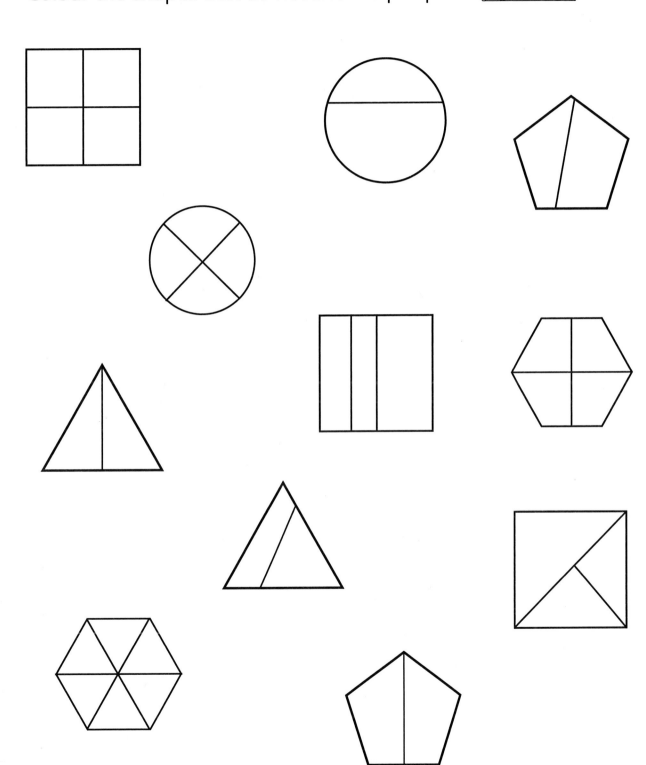

Exploring Fractions

A **fraction** shows equal parts of a whole.

Numerator: the number that shows the number of parts being counted.

Denominator: the number that shows the total number of equal parts in the whole.

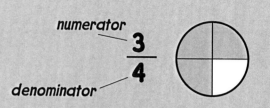

numerator $\dfrac{3}{4}$ denominator

This means 3 out of 4 parts are shaded.

1 Circle the numerator (red ⊳ .
Circle the denominator (green ⊳ .

a $\dfrac{2}{3}$ **b** $\dfrac{4}{6}$ **c** $\dfrac{1}{2}$ **d** $\dfrac{3}{4}$

2 Write a fraction using the given numerator and denominator.

a Numerator: 4
Denominator: 6

_____

b Numerator: 2
Denominator: 4

_____

c Numerator: 1
Denominator: 3

_____

3 Write how many parts each circle is divided into.

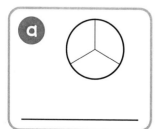

_____

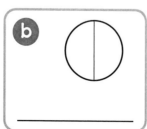

_____

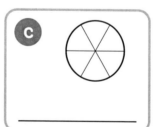

_____

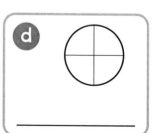

_____

I can identify fractions.

Exploring Sets

A **set** is a collection of items forming a group.

There are 4 tents. 3 tents are grey and 1 is white. What is the fraction of grey tents?

$$\frac{3}{4}$$

Write a fraction for the given set.

Colour the pictures to help.

1 There are 3 shells. 2 shells are brown and 1 is pink. What is the fraction of pink shells?

———

2 There are 6 glasses. 2 glasses are orange. 3 glasses are red, and 1 is blue. What is the fraction of red glasses?

———

3 There are 2 apples. 1 apple is red and 1 is green. What is the fraction of red apples?

———

I can identify fractions in sets.

Exploring Halves

Halves are the 2 equal parts of a whole.

One whole	Halves	$\frac{1}{2}$ of the parts are shaded

1 Colour one half of the parts.

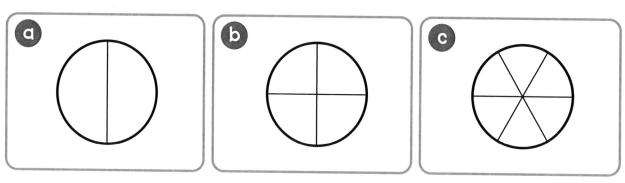

A **set** is a collection of items forming a group.

2 Colour one half of each set.

I can identify halves.

Exploring Fourths

Fourths are the 4 equal parts of a whole.

One whole   Fourths $\frac{1}{4}$ of the parts are shaded

1 Colour the correct portion of the fourths.

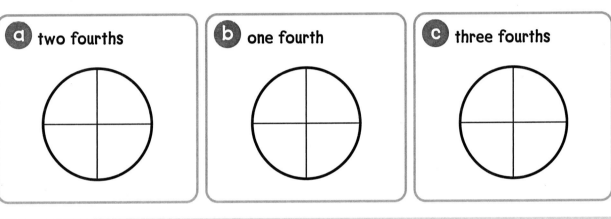

a two fourths   **b** one fourth   **c** three fourths

A **set** is a collection of items forming a group.

2 Colour one fourth of each set.

a
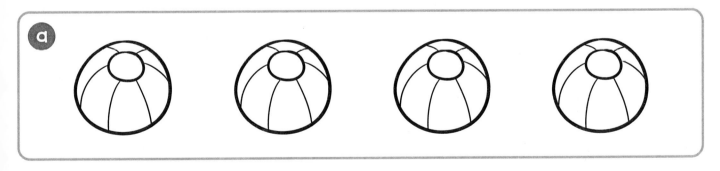

b
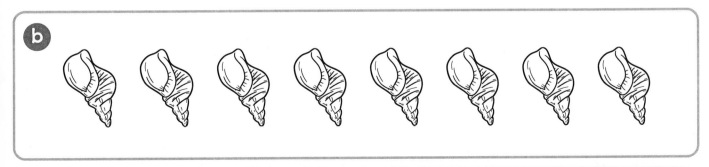

Exploring Thirds

Thirds are the 3 equal parts of a whole.

One whole

Thirds

$\frac{1}{3}$ **of the parts are shaded**

1 Colour the correct portion of the thirds.

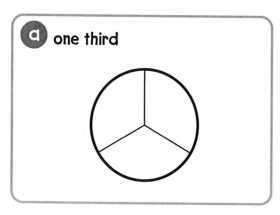

a one third

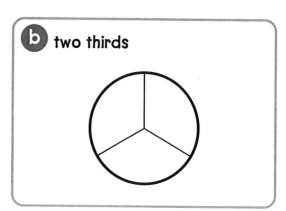

b two thirds

A set is a collection of items forming a group.

2 Colour one third of each set.

a

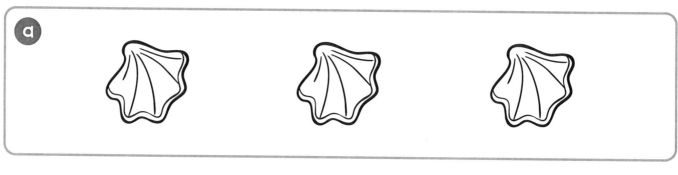

b

I can identify thirds.

Exploring Sixths

Sixths are the 6 equal parts of a whole.

One whole

Sixths

$\frac{1}{6}$ **of the parts are shaded**

1 Colour the correct portion of the sixths.

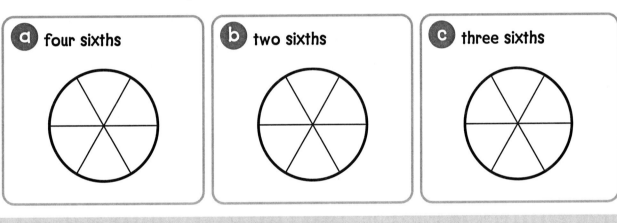

a four sixths

b two sixths

c three sixths

A set is a collection of items forming a group.

2 Colour one sixth of each set.

a

b

Identifying Fractions

1 Circle the correct fraction for the shaded part of the shape.

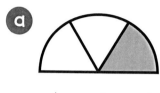

$\dfrac{1}{2}$ $\dfrac{1}{3}$ $\dfrac{1}{4}$

b

$\dfrac{1}{2}$ $\dfrac{1}{3}$ $\dfrac{1}{4}$

c

$\dfrac{1}{2}$ $\dfrac{1}{3}$ $\dfrac{1}{4}$

2 Write the correct fraction for the shaded part of the shape.

a 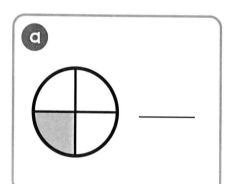 _____

b 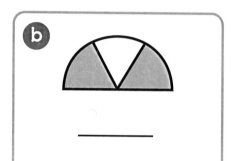 _____

c 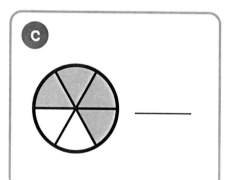 _____

d 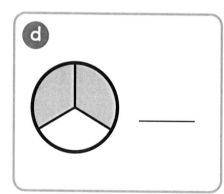 _____

e 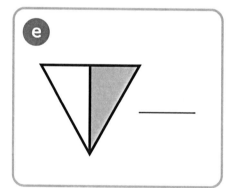 _____

f 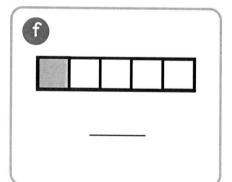 _____

g 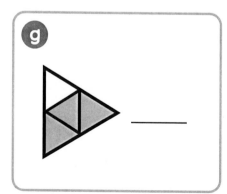 _____

h 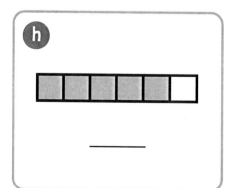 _____

i 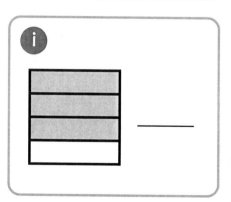 _____

I can identify fractions.

Colour the Fractions

Read the instructions. Colour the fractions.

1
Colour $\frac{1}{4}$ blue.
Colour $\frac{1}{4}$ red.
Colour $\frac{1}{4}$ yellow.
Colour $\frac{1}{4}$ green.

2
Colour $\frac{1}{2}$ red.
Colour $\frac{1}{2}$ green.
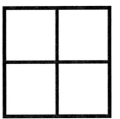

3
Colour $\frac{1}{4}$ purple.
Colour $\frac{1}{4}$ red.
Colour $\frac{2}{4}$ green.

4
Colour $\frac{2}{6}$ red.
Colour $\frac{3}{6}$ blue.
Colour $\frac{1}{6}$ green.

5
Colour $\frac{1}{3}$ orange.
Colour $\frac{2}{3}$ purple.

6
Colour $\frac{1}{3}$ blue.
Colour $\frac{1}{3}$ green.
Colour $\frac{1}{3}$ red.
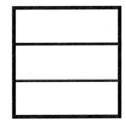

7
Colour $\frac{3}{4}$ of the group orange.

8
Colour $\frac{1}{3}$ of the group yellow.

Exploring Fraction Bars

1 Colour the **one whole** fraction bar **yellow**.
Colour the **one half** fraction bars **blue**.
Colour the **one third** fraction bars **green**.
Colour the **one quarter** fraction bars **red**.

one whole 1			
one half $\frac{1}{2}$		one half $\frac{1}{2}$	
one third $\frac{1}{3}$	one third $\frac{1}{3}$	one third $\frac{1}{3}$	
one quarter $\frac{1}{4}$	one quarter $\frac{1}{4}$	one quarter $\frac{1}{4}$	one quarter $\frac{1}{4}$
one sixth $\frac{1}{6}$	one sixth $\frac{1}{6}$	one sixth $\frac{1}{6}$	one sixth $\frac{1}{6}$	one sixth $\frac{1}{6}$	one sixth $\frac{1}{6}$

2 Circle the fraction that is larger.

a one whole   or   one half

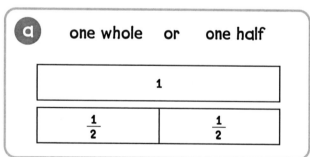

b $\frac{1}{4}$ or $\frac{1}{3}$

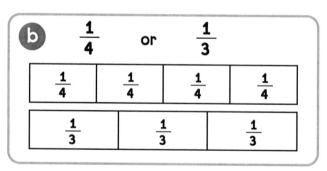

c one half   or   one sixth

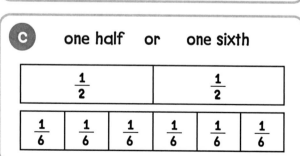

d $\frac{1}{3}$ or $\frac{1}{2}$

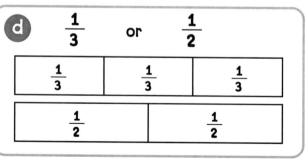

I can identify fraction bars.

Exploring Fraction Bars (continued)

3 Write a fraction to represent the shaded fraction bar.

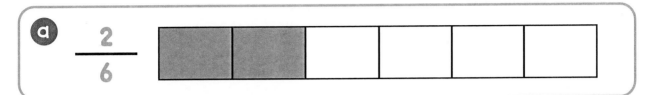

a $\dfrac{2}{6}$

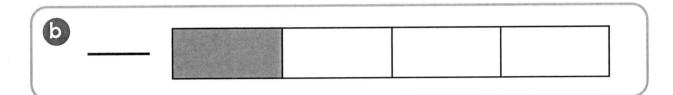

b _____

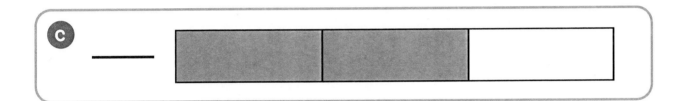

c _____

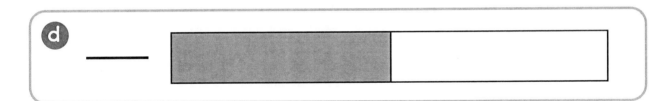

d _____

4 Colour the fraction bar to represent the fraction.

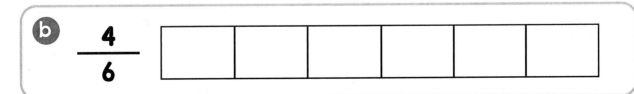

a $\dfrac{3}{4}$

b $\dfrac{4}{6}$

Exploring Equal Amounts

1 Colour one third. Colour one fourth.

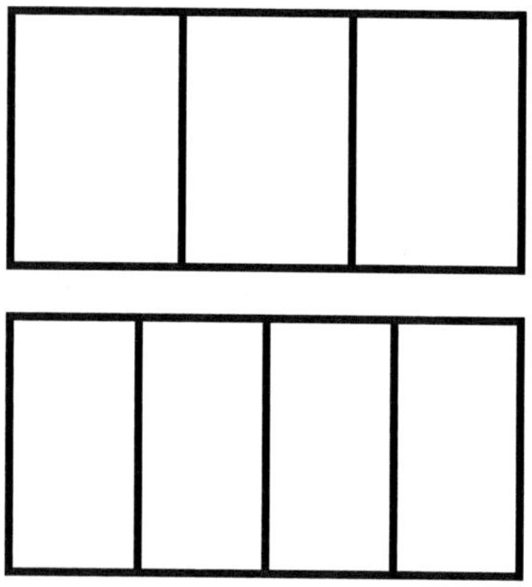

Are the fractions the same size?

YES   **NO**

2 Colour one third. Colour two sixths.

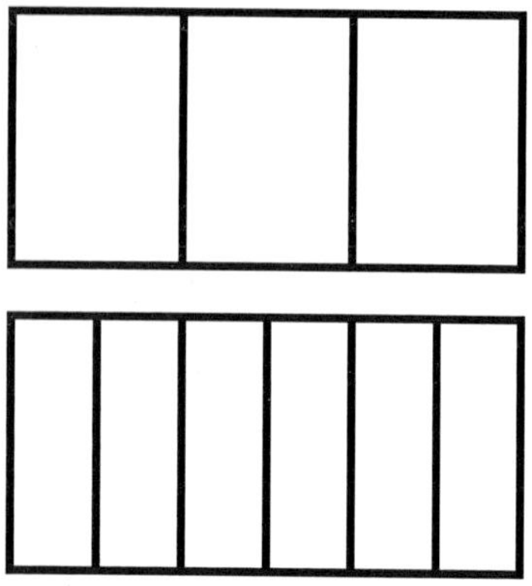

Are the fractions the same size?

YES   **NO**

3 Colour one half. Colour one fourth.

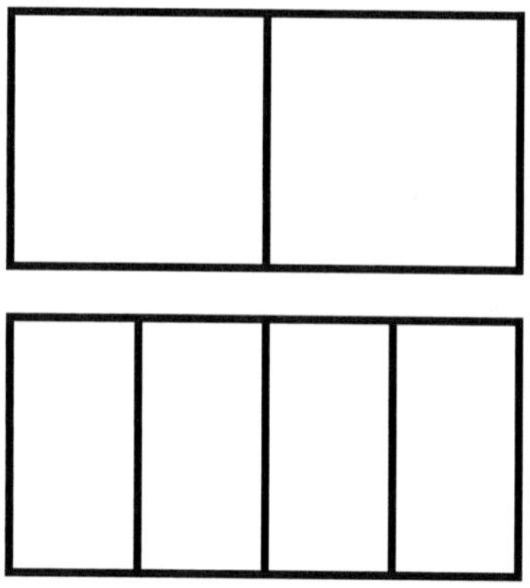

Are the fractions the same size?

YES   **NO**

I can identify equal amounts.

Exploring Equal Amounts (continued)

4 Colour one half. Colour one third.

Are the fractions the same size?

YES   NO

5 Colour one half. Colour two fourths.

Are the fractions the same size?

YES   NO

6 Colour two thirds. Colour one sixth.

Are the fractions the same size?

YES   NO

Fraction Word Problems

Solve the word problems. Write the correct fraction.

  Margo counts 4 mailboxes on her street. 3 mailboxes are green. What fraction of the mailboxes are green?

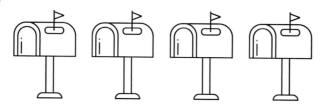

_____ of the mailboxes are green.

  Ivan has 2 granola bars. He gives 1 granola bar to his friend. What fraction of the granola bars did Ivan give away?

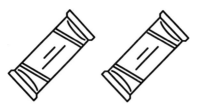

_____ of the granola bars were given away.

  Twila has 3 juice boxes. She gives 2 juice boxes to her brother. What fraction of the juice boxes did Twila give away?

_____ of the juice boxes were given away.

  I can solve fraction word problems.

Fair Sharing

Fair sharing in math means making sure that everyone gets an equal amount of something when it is divided.

Are the friends equally sharing the items? Circle **YES** or **NO**.

YES OR NO

YES OR NO

YES OR NO

Exploring Fair Shares

A **remainder** is the amount left over when items cannot be equally shared.

Circle the equal share each child will get.

1 If there are 3 children...

Are there any remainders? YES   NO

2 If there are 2 children...

Are there any remainders? YES   NO

3 If there are 6 children...

Are there any remainders? YES   NO

4 If there are 4 children...

Are there any remainders? YES   NO

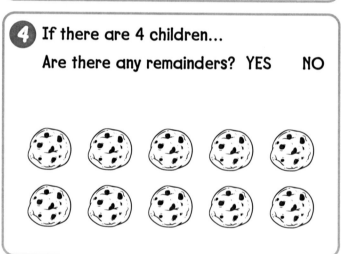

5 If there are 3 children...

Are there any remainders? YES   NO

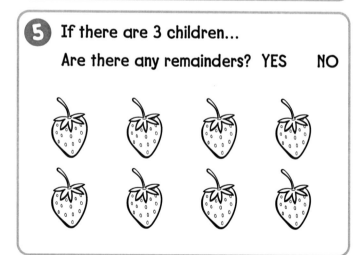

6 If there are 2 children...

Are there any remainders? YES   NO

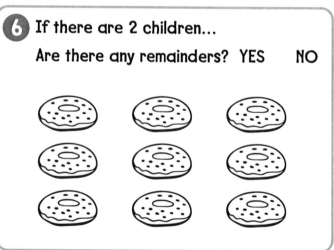

I can identify fair sharing with remainders.

Fair Share Word Problems

Sometimes there are not enough whole pieces to equally share.

If two people are sharing 3 cupcakes, they can each have one full cupcake, but that leaves one left over.

The leftover cupcake can be divided in half and shared equally.

Each person now gets one and a half cupcakes.

1 Solve the problem. Use the picture to help you.

Two friends want to share 5 pies. How many whole pies will each friend get? _____
How can the remainder be shared?

Fair Share Word Problems (continued)

2 Solve the problem. Use the picture to help you.

a Three friends want to share 7 pizzas. How many whole pizzas will each friend get? How can the remainder be shared?

b Four friends want to share 5 cakes. How many whole cakes will each friend get? How can the remainder be shared? Cut the cake into equal slices.

I can solve fair share word problems.

Fair Share Word Problems (continued)

3 Draw each fraction to solve the problem.

a Jack eats $\frac{1}{3}$ of a cookie.

Tia eats $\frac{2}{6}$ of a cookie.

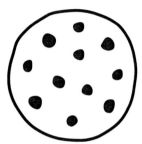

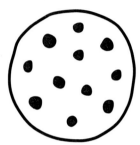

Do Jack and Tia eat the same amount of cookie?

YES OR NO

b Aimee eats $\frac{1}{2}$ of a pie.

Yuri eats $\frac{2}{4}$ of a pie.

Do Aimee and Yuri eat the same amount of pie?

YES OR NO

Show What You Know!

1 Circle the shapes that **do not** show equal parts.

    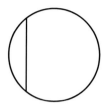

2 Colour a fraction equal to the one shown.

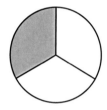 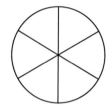

3 Identify what fraction is shaded in the shape.

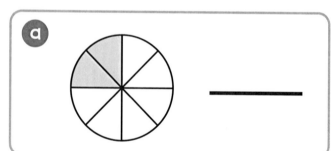

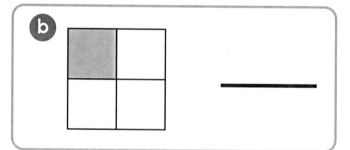

4 Circle the equal share each child will get.

a If there are 5 children...

Are there any remainders?   YES   NO

b If there are 3 children...

Are there any remainders?   YES   NO

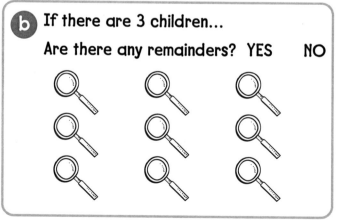

Show What You Know! (continued)

5 Read the instructions. Colour the fractions.

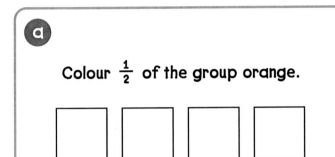

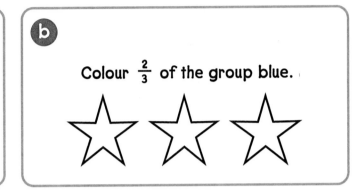

6 Solve the problem. Draw pictures to help you.

There are 10 cookies in the jar and 4 students to share them. How many cookies can each student get fairly? How many cookies are left over?

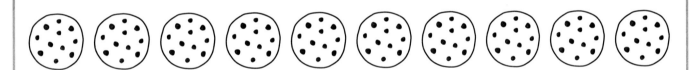

There are _____ cookies left over.

7 Circle the fraction that is larger.

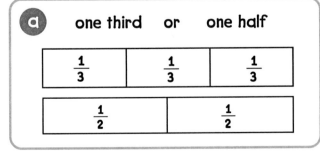

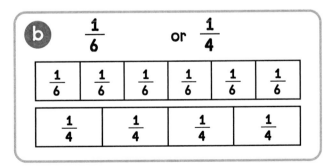

I Can Checklist:
Operations

 Use the properties of addition and subtraction, and the relationships between addition and multiplication and between subtraction and division, to solve problems and check calculations. For example,

- *I can use addition to solve a multiplication problem, and subtraction to solve a division problem.*
- *I can check my subtraction answers by adding.*

 Recall and demonstrate addition facts for numbers up to 20, and related subtraction facts. For example,

- *I can remember and show that 15 + 5 equals 20 and that 20 – 5 equals 15.*

 Use mental math strategies, including estimation, to add and subtract whole numbers that add up to no more than 50, and explain the strategies used. For example,

- *I can estimate the answer to 23 + 15 by rounding each number to the nearest ten, then adding.*

 Use objects, diagrams, and equations to represent, describe, and solve situations involving addition and subtraction of whole numbers that add up to no more than 100. For example,

- *I can use blocks to add 35 and 45 together to make 80.*
- *I can use a number line to subtract 25 from 75.*

 Represent multiplication as repeated equal groups, including groups of one half and one fourth, and solve related problems using various tools and drawings. For example,

- *I can draw 3 groups of 4 apples to represent 3 × 4 = 12.*
- *I can represent 2 groups of half a pizza to show that 2 × ¹/₂ equals 1 whole pizza.*

 Represent division of up to 12 items as the equal sharing of a quantity, and solve related problems, using various tools and drawings. For example,

- *I can draw circles or use counters to show that 12 cookies divided by 4 friends means each friend gets 3 cookies.*

Addition Strategies

Plus Zero

Add 0 to a number and the number stays the same.

$5 + 0 = 5$

Turn Around

Add the numbers in any order and the total stays the same.

$2 + 1 = 3$ or $1 + 2 = 3$

Friends of Ten

There are six sets of number pairs that equal 10.

$10 + 0 = 10$ $7 + 3 = 10$

$9 + 1 = 10$ $6 + 4 = 10$

$8 + 2 = 10$ $5 + 5 = 10$

Doubles Plus 1

Double the number and add one more.

$3 + 4 = 3 + 3 + 1$

Doubles

Add the number to itself and that number doubles.

$4 + 4 = 8$

Count On

Count on to add small numbers such as 1, 2, or 3.

$11 + 2 = ?$ Count 11, 12, 13

$11 + 2 = 13$

Draw a Picture

$3 + 2 = 5$

Doubles Strategy for Addition

A number plus itself is doubled.

$$2 + 2 = 4$$

Use the doubles strategy to solve.

1 4 + 4 =

2 1 + 1 =

3 6 + 6 =

4 9 + 9 =

5 2 + 2 =

6 7 + 7 =

7 8 + 8 =

8 3 + 3 =

9 5 + 5 =

10 10 + 10 =

I can add using doubles.

Doubles Plus 1 Strategy for Addition

A number plus itself is doubled. Then, add one more.

$$4 + 5 = 4 + 4 + 1$$

Use the doubles plus 1 strategy to solve.

1 1 + 2 =

2 8 + 9 =

3 6 + 7 =

4 4 + 5 =

5 3 + 4 =

6 9 + 10 =

7 2 + 3 =

8 7 + 8 =

9 5 + 6 =

10 10 + 11 =

Draw a Picture Strategy for Addition

Draw shapes for each number, than add all the shapes to find the total.

$$\bullet\bullet\atop\bullet\bullet \; + \; \bullet\bullet\bullet\atop\bullet\bullet\bullet \; = \; 10$$

4 + 6 = 10

Draw a picture to add.

1 2 + 8

2 9 + 5

3 4 + 7

4 6 + 8

✓ I can add using pictures.

Exploring Estimation

Estimation is a mental math strategy for addition and subtraction.

For example,
Round each number to the nearest ten, then add.

Rounding the numbers gives an approximate total.

$$
\begin{array}{r}
18 \longrightarrow 20 \\
+\ 23 \longrightarrow +\ 20 \\
\hline
40
\end{array}
$$

1 Round each number to the nearest ten, then add or subtract.

a
$$
\begin{array}{r}
8 \\
+\ 12
\end{array}
\longrightarrow
+\ \underline{}
$$

b
$$
\begin{array}{r}
29 \\
+\ 13
\end{array}
\longrightarrow
+\ \underline{}
$$

c
$$
\begin{array}{r}
22 \\
-\ 7
\end{array}
\longrightarrow
-\ \underline{}
$$

d
$$
\begin{array}{r}
26 \\
-\ 8
\end{array}
\longrightarrow
-\ \underline{}
$$

e
$$
\begin{array}{r}
9 \\
+\ 35
\end{array}
\longrightarrow
+\ \underline{}
$$

f
$$
\begin{array}{r}
15 \\
+\ 26
\end{array}
\longrightarrow
+\ \underline{}
$$

2 Estimate the total and circle the matching description.

a 17 + 32   more than 50   less than 50

b 56 – 28   more than 20   less than 20

c 44 + 35   more than 70   less than 70

Adding Tens and Ones

A number can be broken down into a sum of tens and ones.

23 = 10 + 10 + 1 + 1 + 1

1 Break down the number as a sum of tens and ones.

a 31 =

b 14 =

2 43 is the same as 40 + 3. Write each number the same way.

a 56 =

b 79 =

c 95 =

d 38 =

3 Add the tens and ones.

a 40 + 5 =

b 20 + 8 =

c 50 + 7 =

d 60 + 2 =

e 6 + 2 =

60 + 20 =

f 8 + 1 =

80 + 10 =

g 3 + 5 =

30 + 50 =

h 4 + 3 =

40 + 30 =

I can add tens Tend ones.

Adding Tens and Ones (continued)

Add two-digit numbers by lining up the tens and ones.

$$15 = 10 + 5$$
$$+42 = 40 + 2$$
$$57 \leftarrow 50 + 7$$

4 Separate the tens and ones to add.

a
$$33 = 30 + \boxed{}$$
$$+ 44 = 40 + \boxed{}$$
$$\boxed{} \leftarrow 70 + \boxed{}$$

b
$$41 = 40 + \boxed{}$$
$$+ 37 = 30 + \boxed{}$$
$$\boxed{} \leftarrow 70 + \boxed{}$$

c
$$56 = \boxed{} + \boxed{}$$
$$+ 13 = \boxed{} + \boxed{}$$
$$\boxed{} \leftarrow \boxed{} + \boxed{}$$

d
$$12 = \boxed{} + \boxed{}$$
$$+ 25 = \boxed{} + \boxed{}$$
$$\boxed{} \leftarrow \boxed{} + \boxed{}$$

e
$$71 = \boxed{} + \boxed{}$$
$$+ 26 = \boxed{} + \boxed{}$$
$$\boxed{} \leftarrow \boxed{} + \boxed{}$$

f
$$63 = \boxed{} + \boxed{}$$
$$+ 14 = \boxed{} + \boxed{}$$
$$\boxed{} \leftarrow \boxed{} + \boxed{}$$

g
$$27 = \boxed{} + \boxed{}$$
$$+ 31 = \boxed{} + \boxed{}$$
$$\boxed{} \leftarrow \boxed{} + \boxed{}$$

h
$$84 = \boxed{} + \boxed{}$$
$$+ 15 = \boxed{} + \boxed{}$$
$$\boxed{} \leftarrow \boxed{} + \boxed{}$$

Find the Missing Number

Fill in the missing number.

1
```
    1 5
+ [   ]
-------
    2 0
```

2
```
  [   ]
+ 1 1
-------
  1 4
```

3
```
      8
+ [   ]
-------
  1 0
```

4
```
    1 2
+ [   ]
-------
  1 9
```

5
```
  [   ]
+   7
-------
  1 4
```

6
```
    1 7
+ [   ]
-------
  2 0
```

7
```
      4
+ [   ]
-------
  1 6
```

8
```
  [   ]
+   9
-------
  1 3
```

9
```
      5
+ [   ]
-------
  1 8
```

10
```
  [   ]
+ 1 2
-------
  1 5
```

11
```
    1 4
+ [   ]
-------
  1 9
```

12
```
  [   ]
+   7
-------
  1 1
```

13
```
  [   ]
+ 1 0
-------
  1 7
```

14
```
      2
+ [   ]
-------
  1 6
```

15
```
      6
+ [   ]
-------
  1 3
```

16
```
  [   ]
+   2
-------
      9
```

I can find the missing number.

Addition Riddle

Find the sums. Solve the riddle. (Hint: Not all of the letters are used.)

A	C	D	E	H
$\begin{array}{r}10\\ +\ 9\\\hline\end{array}$	$\begin{array}{r}7\\ +\ 6\\\hline\end{array}$	$\begin{array}{r}5\\ +\ 1\\\hline\end{array}$	$\begin{array}{r}9\\ +\ 7\\\hline\end{array}$	$\begin{array}{r}10\\ +\ 7\\\hline\end{array}$
I	**K**	**L**	**N**	**O**
$\begin{array}{r}8\\ +\ 4\\\hline\end{array}$	$\begin{array}{r}9\\ +\ 9\\\hline\end{array}$	$\begin{array}{r}3\\ +\ 3\\\hline\end{array}$	$\begin{array}{r}8\\ +\ 6\\\hline\end{array}$	$\begin{array}{r}5\\ +\ 4\\\hline\end{array}$
P	**R**	**S**	**T**	**U**
$\begin{array}{r}8\\ +\ 2\\\hline\end{array}$	$\begin{array}{r}10\\ +\ 10\\\hline\end{array}$	$\begin{array}{r}9\\ +\ 2\\\hline\end{array}$	$\begin{array}{r}7\\ +\ 1\\\hline\end{array}$	$\begin{array}{r}3\\ +\ 2\\\hline\end{array}$
V	**W**	**X**	**Y**	**Z**
$\begin{array}{r}9\\ +\ 6\\\hline\end{array}$	$\begin{array}{r}4\\ +\ 3\\\hline\end{array}$	$\begin{array}{r}5\\ +\ 6\\\hline\end{array}$	$\begin{array}{r}2\\ +\ 2\\\hline\end{array}$	$\begin{array}{r}1\\ +\ 8\\\hline\end{array}$

Why did the turkey cross the road?

___ ___ / ___ ___ ___ ___ ___ / ___ ___
8 9   10 20 9 15 16   17 16

___ ___ ___ ___ ' ___ / ___ ___ ___ ___ ___ ___ ___ !
7 19 11 14   8   13 17 12 13 18 16 14

Two-Digit Addition Without Regrouping

Line up the **ones** and **tens**.

Add the **ones**.

```
  1 | 5
+ 2 | 4
----+---
    | 9
```

Next, add the **tens**.

```
  1 | 5
+ 2 | 4
----+---
  3 | 9
```

1 Use the tens and ones chart to add. Shade the ones column in red. Shade the tens column in yellow.

a
tens	ones
2	4
+ 6	2

b
tens	ones
4	3
+ 4	4

c
tens	ones
6	8
+ 1	1

d
tens	ones
3	5
+ 2	2

e
```
  1 | 7
+ 4 | 1
```

f
```
  8 | 5
+ 1 | 0
```

g
```
  4 | 1
+ 2 | 6
```

h
```
  1 | 9
+ 5 | 0
```

2 There were 43 dog treats in one jar. In another jar, there are 52 dog treats. How many dog treats are there in total?

I can add two-digit numbers without regrouping. © Chalkboard Publishing Inc

Two-Digit Addition Without Regrouping (continued)

3 Find the sums. Solve the riddle. (Hint: Not all of the letters are used.)

A 13 + 53	**B** 27 + 21	**D** 20 + 41	**E** 31 + 36	**G** 53 + 32	**H** 11 + 41
I 51 + 26	**L** 42 + 34	**M** 74 + 14	**N** 36 + 43	**O** 41 + 22	**P** 22 + 51
Q 20 + 60	**R** 77 + 20	**S** 56 + 43	**T** 12 + 21	**U** 20 + 30	**V** 12 + 45
W 22 + 32	**Z** 31 + 44				

How does the solar system hold up its pants?

___ ___ ___ ___ / ___ ___ /
54 77 33 52   66 79

___ ___ ___ ___ ___ ___ ___ ___ / ___ ___ ___ ___ !
66 99 33 67 97 63 77 61   48 67 76 33

Two-Digit Addition With Regrouping

Step 1. Add the ones. 6 + 7 = 13

      Regroup 13 ones as 1 ten and 3 ones.

Step 2. Add the tens. 1 + 2 + 1 = 4

tens	ones
1	
2	6
+ 1	7
4	3

1 Use the tens and ones chart to add. Shade the ones column in blue. Shade the tens column in green.

a

tens	ones
☐	
6	5
+ 2	8

b

tens	ones
☐	
4	9
+ 2	7

c

tens	ones
☐	
2	3
+ 3	9

d

tens	ones
☐	
2	1
+ 4	9

e

☐	
7	2
+ 1	8

f

☐	
3	9
+ 2	6

g

☐	
5	8
+ 1	4

h

☐	
6	4
+ 2	7

2 There are 46 people in one line at the amusement park. In another line, there are 38 people. How many people are in line at the amusement park in total?

I can add two-digit numbers with regrouping. © Chalkboard Publishing Inc

Two-Digit Addition With Regrouping (continued)

3 Find the sums. Solve the riddle. Hint: Not all of the letters are used.

A	B	C	D	E	G
14 + 28	13 + 49	39 + 11	38 + 8	19 + 17	28 + 32

H	I	J	K	L	M
66 + 9	63 + 18	54 + 7	36 + 58	48 + 9	59 + 19

N	O	P	R	S	T
57 + 6	24 + 49	57 + 27	34 + 46	28 + 27	16 + 35

U	V	W	X	Y	Z
49 + 42	35 + 35	66 + 26	19 + 76	77 + 13	24 + 47

Why didn't the astronaut like the restaurant?

____ ____ / ____ ____ ____ / ____ ____
81 51   75 42 46   63 73

____ ____ ____ ____ ____ ____ ____ ____ ____ ____ !
42 51 78 73 55 84 75 36 80 36

Subtraction Strategies

Minus Zero

Subtract 0 from a number and the number stays the same.

$8 - 0 = 8$

Friends of Ten

If you know the tens partner, then you know the related subtraction fact.

$9 + 1 = 10$ or $10 - 1 = 9$

A Number Minus Itself

Subtract a number from itself and the result is 0.

$7 - 7 = 0$

Doubles

If you know the doubles fact, then you know the related subtraction fact.

$2 + 2 = 4$ or $4 - 2 = 2$

Count Backward

Count back to take away small numbers such as 1, 2, or 3.

11, 10, 9

$11 - 2 = ?$

$11 - 2 = 9$

Use a Number Line

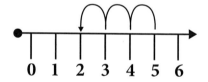

$5 - 3 = ?$ $5 - 3 = 2$

Think Addition

Every subtraction problem can be solved as an addition problem.

$4 + 1 = 5$ or $5 - 1 = 4$

Draw a Picture

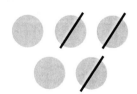

$5 - 3 = 2$

Mental Math Strategies for Subtraction

15 - 8

I know **8 + 2 = 10**.

So I add **2** to each number.

17 - 10

Then I subtract to get the answer.

17 - 10 = 7

Add to the numbers to make tens. Subtract the numbers.

1   14 − 9

2   12 − 6

3   18 − 5

4   16 − 4

Draw a Picture Strategy for Subtraction

Draw shapes for the first number.
Cross out the second number, then count the remaining shapes for the total.

$8 - 3 = 5$

Draw a picture to subtract.

1 $6 - 4$

2 $10 - 3$

3 $9 - 5$

4 $4 - 2$

I can subtract using pictures. © Chalkboard Publishing Inc

Doubles Strategy for Subtraction

If you know the doubles fact, then you know the related subtraction fact!

$$3 + 3 = 6 \quad \text{so} \quad 6 - 3 = 3$$

Use the doubles strategy to solve.

1 $14 - 7 =$

2 $6 - 3 =$

3 $12 - 6 =$

4 $8 - 4 =$

5 $10 - 5 =$

6 $2 - 1 =$

7 $16 - 8 =$

8 $20 - 10 =$

9 $4 - 2 =$

10 $18 - 9 =$

Number Line Strategy for Subtraction

Count down on a number line to subtract.

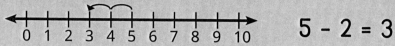

5 - 2 = 3

Use the number line strategy to solve.

1 10 − 4 =

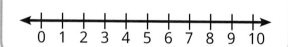

2 8 − 5 =

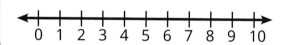

3 7 − 1 =

4 4 − 3 =

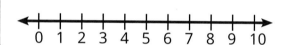

5 6 − 2 =

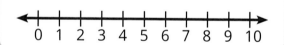

6 9 − 7 =

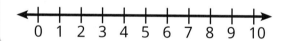

7 2 − 1 =

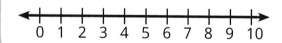

8 10 − 5 =

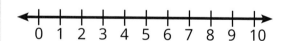

9 5 − 4 =

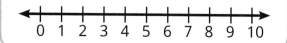

10 3 − 1 =

I can subtract using number lines.

Checking Subtraction by Using Addition

Use addition to check your subtraction answers.

Add the subtraction answer to the problem to see if you get the same result!

$$
\begin{array}{r} 3\ 5 \\ -\ 2\ 4 \\ \hline 1\ 1 \end{array}
\qquad
\begin{array}{r} 1\ 1 \\ +\ 2\ 4 \\ \hline 3\ 5 \end{array}
$$

Subtract. Then use addition to check your answer.

1

subtract	check
36	☐
− 12	+ 16
☐	☐

2

subtract	check
47	☐
− 22	+ 27
☐	☐

3

subtract	check
65	☐
− 31	+ 35
☐	☐

4

subtract	check
29	☐
− 14	+ 14
☐	☐

5

subtract	check
57	☐
− 42	+ 42
☐	☐

6

subtract	check
75	☐
− 30	+ 30
☐	☐

Find the Missing Number

Fill in the missing number.

1
$$16 - \boxed{} = 10$$

2
$$\boxed{} - 6 = 12$$

3
$$16 - \boxed{} = 5$$

4
$$13 - \boxed{} = 7$$

5
$$\boxed{} - 8 = 4$$

6
$$14 - \boxed{} = 5$$

7
$$17 - \boxed{} = 15$$

8
$$\boxed{} - 9 = 4$$

9
$$10 - \boxed{} = 1$$

10
$$\boxed{} - 12 = 7$$

11
$$18 - \boxed{} = 10$$

12
$$\boxed{} - 12 = 3$$

13
$$\boxed{} - 9 = 9$$

14
$$16 - \boxed{} = 4$$

15
$$11 - \boxed{} = 5$$

16
$$\boxed{} - 5 = 14$$

I can find the missing number.

Subtraction Riddle

Find the differences. Solve the riddle. Hint: Not all the letters are used.

A	B	C	D	E
20 − 0	17 − 9	19 − 2	14 − 7	18 − 0
F 10 − 5	**G** 13 − 7	**H** 19 − 3	**I** 20 − 1	**J** 13 − 4
K 19 − 6	**L** 9 − 5	**N** 14 − 2	**O** 8 − 6	**P** 15 − 4
R 2 − 1	**T** 19 − 4	**U** 12 − 9	**W** 15 − 5	**Y** 18 − 4

What do you get when you cross a parrot with a shark?

___ / ___ ___ ___ ___ / ___ ___ ___ ___ / ___ ___ ___ ___ /
20   8 19 1 7   15 16 20 15   10 19 4 4

___ ___ ___ ___ / ___ ___ ___ ___ / ___ ___ ___ / ___ ___ ___ !
15 20 4 13   14 2 3 1   18 20 1   2 5 5

Two-Digit Subtraction Without Regrouping

Line up the **ones** and **tens**.

Subtract the **ones**.	Next, subtract the **tens**.
$\begin{array}{c|c} 8 & 7 \\ -\ 3 & 5 \\ \hline & 2 \end{array}$	$\begin{array}{c|c} 8 & 7 \\ -\ 3 & 5 \\ \hline 5 & 2 \end{array}$

1 Use the tens and ones chart to subtract. Shade the ones column in red. Shade the tens column in yellow.

a

tens	ones
5	3
− 4	0

b

tens	ones
9	7
− 7	3

c

tens	ones
6	6
− 3	4

d

tens	ones
3	3
− 2	1

e

9	5
− 4	1

f

7	8
− 1	1

g

8	4
− 5	2

h

2	9
− 1	7

2 There are 87 flowers in a field. 52 flowers are picked by visitors. How many flowers are left in the field?

I can subtract two-digits without regrouping. © Chalkboard Publishing Inc

Two-Digit Subtraction Without Regrouping (continued)

3 Find the sums. Solve the riddle. Hint: Not all the letters are used.

A	B	C	D	E
49 − 24	51 − 10	45 − 15	98 − 54	66 − 23
H	**I**	**L**	**M**	**P**
98 − 67	55 − 34	57 − 24	38 − 18	77 − 63
R	**S**	**T**	**U**	**Y**
64 − 53	48 − 16	75 − 25	87 − 45	39 − 29

 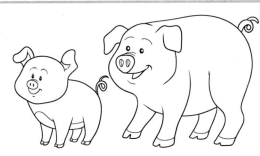

How can you fit more pigs on a farm?

___ ___ ___ ___ ___ / ___ / ___ ___ ___ /
41 42 21 33 44   25   32 50 10

___ ___ ___ ___ ___ ___ ___ !
32 30 11 25 14 43 11

Two-Digit Subtraction With Regrouping

Line up the ones and tens.

Subtract the ones.

You cannot take 9 from 2.

So, trade 1 ten from the tens for 10 ones in the ones.

Now there are 12 ones.

Write the ones.

Then write the tens.

tens	ones
3	12
4̸	2̸
- 3	9
0	3

1 Use the tens and ones chart to subtract. Shade the ones column in red. Shade the tens column in green.

a

tens	ones
□	□
9	4
- 6	5

b

tens	ones
□	□
8	4
- 4	6

c

tens	ones
□	□
7	2
- 3	5

d

tens	ones
□	□
6	3
- 2	5

e

□	□
5	5
- 2	7

f

□	□
7	6
- 3	9

g

□	□
4	0
- 2	2

h

□	□
9	1
- 1	3

2 There are 41 cupcakes at a bake sale. 28 cupcakes are sold during the sale. How many cupcakes are left?

I can subtract two-digit numbers with regrouping. © Chalkboard Publishing Inc

Two-Digit Subtraction With Regrouping (continued)

3 Find the sums. Solve the riddle.

A $\begin{array}{r} 58 \\ -\ 29 \\ \hline \end{array}$	**B** $\begin{array}{r} 76 \\ -\ 38 \\ \hline \end{array}$	**C** $\begin{array}{r} 38 \\ -\ 29 \\ \hline \end{array}$	**D** $\begin{array}{r} 27 \\ -\ 19 \\ \hline \end{array}$	**E** $\begin{array}{r} 66 \\ -\ 49 \\ \hline \end{array}$	**F** $\begin{array}{r} 96 \\ -\ 17 \\ \hline \end{array}$
G $\begin{array}{r} 91 \\ -\ 23 \\ \hline \end{array}$	**H** $\begin{array}{r} 65 \\ -\ 19 \\ \hline \end{array}$	**I** $\begin{array}{r} 72 \\ -\ 36 \\ \hline \end{array}$	**K** $\begin{array}{r} 86 \\ -\ 17 \\ \hline \end{array}$	**N** $\begin{array}{r} 44 \\ -\ 31 \\ \hline \end{array}$	**O** $\begin{array}{r} 55 \\ -\ 18 \\ \hline \end{array}$
R $\begin{array}{r} 72 \\ -\ 45 \\ \hline \end{array}$	**S** $\begin{array}{r} 33 \\ -\ 14 \\ \hline \end{array}$	**T** $\begin{array}{r} 52 \\ -\ 18 \\ \hline \end{array}$	**U** $\begin{array}{r} 90 \\ -\ 72 \\ \hline \end{array}$	**V** $\begin{array}{r} 72 \\ -\ 25 \\ \hline \end{array}$	**Y** $\begin{array}{r} 83 \\ -\ 34 \\ \hline \end{array}$

What animal has more lives than a cat?

___ ___ ___ ___ ___ / ___ ___ ___ ___ ___ ___ ___ /
79   27   37   68   19   38   17   9   29   18   19   17

___ ___ ___ ___ / ___ ___ ___ ___ ___ /
34   46   17   49   9   27   37   29   69

___ ___ ___ ___ ___ / ___ ___ ___ ___ ___ ___ !
17   47   17   27   49   13   36   36   68   46   34

Number Fact Families

1 Read the numbers in the group.
Add or subtract using the three numbers.

a   (7) (9) (16)

_____ + _____ = _____

_____ + _____ = _____

_____ − _____ = _____

_____ − _____ = _____

b   (13) (5) (8)

_____ + _____ = _____

_____ + _____ = _____

_____ − _____ = _____

_____ − _____ = _____

I can add and subtract number fact families.

Number Fact Families (continued)

2 Read the numbers in the group.
   Add or subtract using the three numbers.

a (12) (8) (4)

_____ + _____ = _____

_____ + _____ = _____

_____ − _____ = _____

_____ − _____ = _____

b (9) (19) (10)

_____ + _____ = _____

_____ + _____ = _____

_____ − _____ = _____

_____ − _____ = _____

Addition and Subtraction Problems

1 Decide if you need to add or subtract. Underline any words that help you decide. Solve the problem. Colour **add** or **subtract** to tell what you did.

a

Kevin has 32 hockey cards and 27 baseball cards. How many cards does he have altogether?

add

subtract

Kevin has _____ cards altogether.

b

Missy has 50 yellow buttons and 32 green buttons. How many more yellow buttons does she have than green?

add

subtract

Missy has _____ more yellow buttons than green buttons.

I can solve addition and subtraction word problems. © Chalkboard Publishing Inc

Addition and Subtraction Problems (continued)

2 Decide if you need to add or subtract. Underline any words that help you decide. Solve the problem. Colour **add** or **subtract** to tell what you did.

a

Megan has 45 yellow flowers and 36 purple flowers.
How many flowers does she have altogether?

add

subtract

Megan has _____ flowers altogether.

b

Erin has 63 apples and 32 pears.
How many more apples does she have than pears?

add

subtract

Erin has _____ more apples than pears.

Introducing Multiplication

Look at the groups of 3.

Addition Sentence
There are 3 equal groups.

$3 + 3 + 3 = \underline{9}$

Multiplication Sentence
There are 3 groups of 3.

$3 \times 3 = \underline{9}$

Solve the addition sentence and the multiplication sentence.

1

$5 + 5 = \underline{\hspace{2cm}}$

$2 \times 5 = \underline{\hspace{2cm}}$

2

$2 + 2 + 2 + 2 = \underline{\hspace{2cm}}$

$4 \times 2 = \underline{\hspace{2cm}}$

3

$8 + 8 = \underline{\hspace{2cm}}$

$2 \times 8 = \underline{\hspace{2cm}}$

4

$4 + 4 + 4 = \underline{\hspace{2cm}}$

$3 \times 4 = \underline{\hspace{2cm}}$

I can solve addition and multiplication sentences.

Multiplying Groups

Use groups of objects to multiply.

2 groups of 4

or

2 × 4 = 8

Write and solve the multiplication sentence for the set of pictures.

1

_____ groups of _____

_____ × _____ = _____

2

_____ groups of _____

_____ × _____ = _____

3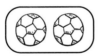
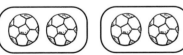

_____ groups of _____

_____ × _____ = _____

4

_____ groups of _____

_____ × _____ = _____

Introducing Division

12 circles are divided into groups of 3.

There are 4 groups of 3.

$$12 \div 3 = 4$$

Write and solve the division sentence for the set of pictures.

1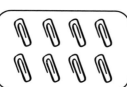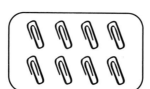

_____ groups of _____

_____ ÷ _____ = _____

2

_____ groups of _____

_____ ÷ _____ = _____

3

_____ groups of _____

_____ ÷ _____ = _____

4

_____ groups of _____

_____ ÷ _____ = _____

I can write and solve division sentences.

Practising Division

Draw groups of circles to help solve the division sentences.

 1

14 ÷ 7 = _____

2

12 ÷ 4 = _____

3

6 ÷ 3 = _____

4

15 ÷ 5 = _____

5

9 ÷ 3 = _____

Multiplication & Division Word Problems

1 Decide if you need to multiply or divide. Underline any words that help you decide. Solve the problem. Colour **multiply** or **divide** to tell what you did.

a

There are 2 plates, and there are 5 cupcakes on each plate. How many cupcakes are there in all?

(multiply)

(divide)

There are _____ cupcakes altogether.

b

Mason has 8 crayons, and he wants to evenly split them into 4 boxes. How many crayons will be in each box?

(multiply)

(divide)

There will be _____ crayons in each box.

I can solve multiplication and division word problems. © Chalkboard Publishing Inc

Multiplication & Division Word Problems (continued)

2 Decide if you need to multiply or divide. Underline any words that help you decide. Solve the problem. Colour **multiply** or **divide** to tell what you did.

---

a

There are 14 cookies, and Teya wants to share them equally among her 2 friends. How many cookies will each friend get?

(multiply)

(divide)

Each friend will get _____ cookies.

---

b

Emma has 3 baskets, and each basket has 4 oranges. How many oranges does Emma have in total?

(multiply)

(divide)

Emma has _____ oranges in total.

I Can Checklist:
Patterning

Identify and describe a variety of patterns involving geometric designs, including patterns found in real-life contexts. For example,

- *I can identify the pattern in a row of houses that are alternately red and blue.*
- *I can point out the pattern in a zebra's stripes, noticing that they alternate between black and white.*
- *I can describe the repeating pattern in the petals of a flower.*

Create and translate patterns using various representations, including shapes and numbers. For example,

- *I can make a pattern using circles and squares, such as circle, square, square, circle, square, square, and so on.*
- *I can create a number pattern such as 2, 4, 6, 8, showing an addition of 2 each time.*
- *I can translate a pattern from shapes to numbers.*

Determine pattern rules and use them to extend patterns, make and justify predictions, and identify missing elements in patterns represented with shapes and numbers. For example,

- *I can figure out that the rule in a pattern of numbers like 3, 6, 9, 12 is 'add 3 each time' and use it to predict the next number (15).*
- *I can determine the missing shape in a pattern.*
- *I can justify my prediction that the next number in the pattern 5, 10, 15, 20 is 25 because the pattern rule is 'add 5 each time.'*

Create and describe patterns to illustrate relationships among whole numbers up to 100. For example,

- *I can create a pattern with numbers up to 100 by skipping counting by 10s: 10, 20, 30, 40, and so on.*
- *I can describe a pattern in the tens and ones places in numbers from 11 to 19, where the tens place is always 1.*
- *I can make a pattern by adding 5 to each number starting from 0 up to 100.*

Patterns in Everyday Life

A **pattern** repeats over and over.
The **core** is the smallest part of a pattern that repeats.

1 Circle the core of each pattern that happens in nature.

a **The Seasons**

b **Day and Night**

2 What patterns do you notice in your everyday life?

Identifying Patterns on a Hundred Chart

1 Start at 2 and count by 2s. Colour each number you count yellow.
Start at 5 and count by 5s. Colour each number you count red.
Start at 10 and count by 10s. Colour each number you count blue.

1	2	3	4	5	6	7	8	9	10
11	12	13	14	15	16	17	18	19	20
21	22	23	24	25	26	27	28	29	30
31	32	33	34	35	36	37	38	39	40
41	42	43	44	45	46	47	48	49	50
51	52	53	54	55	56	57	58	59	60
61	62	63	64	65	66	67	68	69	70
71	72	73	74	75	76	77	78	79	80
81	82	83	84	85	86	87	88	89	90
91	92	93	94	95	96	97	98	99	100

2 What patterns do you see when counting by 2s?

_____

3 What patterns do you see when counting by 5s?

_____

4 What patterns do you see when counting by 10s?

_____

I can identify patterns on a hundred chart.

Exploring Patterns

A **pattern** repeats. The **core** is the smallest part of a pattern that repeats.

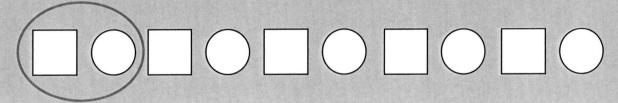

1 Circle the core of each repeating pattern.

a ↑ ⇩ ↑ ⇩ ↑ ⇩ ↑ ⇩ ↑ ⇩ ↑ ⇩

b **B C A B C A B C A B C A**

c **5 6 7 5 6 7 5 6 7 5 6 7**

A **term** is a single piece of a pattern.

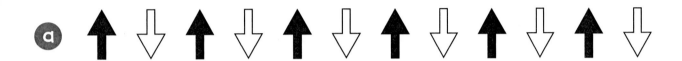

The pattern rule is: Start at 10. Add 10 each time.

2 Write the first 5 terms for each pattern rule.

a Pattern rule: Start at 10. Add 1 each time.

_____, _____, _____, _____, _____

b Pattern rule: Add 20 each time, starting at 100.

_____, _____, _____, _____, _____

I can identify and write patterns.

Translating Patterns

Translating a pattern means changing each term of a pattern into another term while keeping the pattern rule the same. Here is the same pattern in different forms.

Shapes

□ ○ □ ○ □

Sounds

clap, quack, clap, quack, clap

Letters

A B A B A

1 Follow the instructions to translate the pattern.

a Translate using letters.

□ △ □ △ □ △

b Translate using shapes.

A B C A B C A B C

c Translate using sounds.

A B B A B B A B B

d Translate using letters.

△ ○ □ ◇ △ ○ □ ◇

I can translate patterns.

Translating Patterns (continued)

2 Translate the pattern into two different forms.

a **A B B C A B B C**

b ■ ■ ○ ○ ■ ■ ○ ○

c ★ ◇ ◇ ★ ◇ ◇

d ○ △ △ ○ ○ △ △ ○

Extending Patterns

Extending a pattern adds the next terms to the pattern based on the pattern rule.

□ ○ □ ○ □ ○ □ ○ □

Extend the pattern by its next two terms.

1 ■ △ ■ △ ■ △ ■ △ ■ ____ ____

2 1 2 3 1 2 3 1 2 3 ____ ____

3 ○ ☆ ☆ □ ○ ☆ ☆ □ ○ ____ ____

4 3 4 5 6 3 4 5 6 3 4 ____ ____

5 ○ ♡ ♡ ○ ♡ ♡ ○ ♡ ♡ ____ ____

6 ■ △ ● ■ △ ● ■ △ ● ____ ____

7 8 8 3 8 8 3 8 8 3 ____ ____

I can extend patterns.

Naming Patterns

You can name patterns using letters.

○ □ ○ □ ○ □ ○ □

A B A B A B A B

It is an AB pattern. (circle, square, circle, square...)

Name the pattern using letters.

1 ◇ ☆ ○ ◇ ☆ ○ ☆ ○

____ ____ ____ ____ ____ ____ ____ ____

This is an _____ pattern.

2 1 2 2 1 2 2 1 2

____ ____ ____ ____ ____ ____ ____ ____

This is an _____ pattern.

3

____ ____ ____ ____ ____ ____ ____ ____

This is an _____ pattern.

Growing Number Patterns

In a **growing number pattern**, the number increases by the same amount each time.

2 ⁺² 4 ⁺² 6 ⁺² 8 ⁺² 10 ⁺² 12 ⁺² 14 ⁺² 16 ⁺² 18 ⁺² 20

The pattern rule is start at 2 and add 2 each time.

1 Make a growing number pattern.

a **The pattern rule is add 2 each time.**

Start at 8, _____, _____, _____, _____, _____, _____, _____

b **The pattern rule is add 10 each time.**

Start at 15, _____, _____, _____, _____, _____, _____, _____

c **Make your own pattern rule.**

The pattern rule is add _____ each time.

Start at 6, _____, _____, _____, _____, _____, _____, _____

2 Create a growing number pattern.

The pattern rule is add _____ each time.

Start at _____, _____, _____, _____, _____, _____, _____

I can grow number patterns.

Growing Geometric Patterns

1 Continue the growing pattern.

 a

_____   _____   _____

b

_____   _____   _____

2 Draw a growing geometric pattern.

Shrinking Number Patterns

In a **shrinking number pattern,** the number decreases by the same amount each time.

20 $\overset{-2}{}$ 18 $\overset{-2}{}$ 16 $\overset{-2}{}$ 14 $\overset{-2}{}$ 12 $\overset{-2}{}$ 10 $\overset{-2}{}$ 8 $\overset{-2}{}$ 6 $\overset{-2}{}$ 4 $\overset{-2}{}$ 2

The pattern rule is start at 20 and subtract 2 each time.

1 Make a shrinking number pattern.

a **The pattern rule is subtract 2 each time.**

Start at 30, _____, _____, _____, _____, _____, _____, _____

b **The pattern rule is subtract 5 each time.**

Start at 55, _____, _____, _____, _____, _____, _____, _____

c **Make your own pattern rule.**

The pattern rule is subtract _____ each time.

Start at 20, _____, _____, _____, _____, _____, _____, _____

2 Create a shrinking number pattern.

The pattern rule is subtract _____ each time.

Start at , _____, _____, _____, _____, _____, _____, _____

I can shrink number patterns.

Shrinking Geometric Patterns

1 Continue the shrinking pattern.

 a

_____   _____   _____

The pattern rule is start at _____ and subtract _____ each time.

 b

_____   _____   _____

The pattern rule is start at _____ and subtract _____ each time.

2 Draw a shrinking geometric pattern.

Identifying Pattern Changes

An **attribute** of a pattern is a characteristic that is used to describe the pattern, like the size, colour, or position.

Size	Colour	Position

1 How does the pattern change? Circle the attributes. Patterns can have more than one attribute.

a

size
colour
position

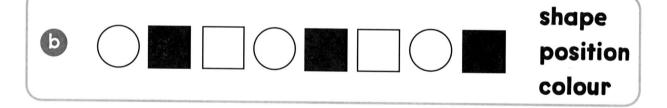

b

shape
position
colour

c

size
colour
shape

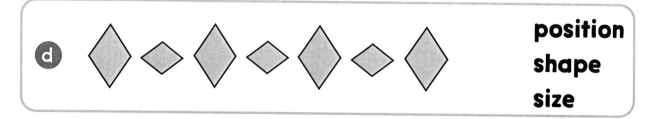

d

position
shape
size

I can identify pattern changes.

Identifying Pattern Changes (continued)

2 How does the pattern change? Circle the attributes.
Patterns can have more than one attribute.

a 2 ⁨⁊⁩ 2 ⁨⁊⁩ 2 ⁨⁊⁩ 2 ⁨⁊⁩ 2 ⁨⁊⁩ 2

size
colour
position

b ↑ ↓ ↑ ↓ ↑ ↓ ↑

shape
position
colour

c ☆ ○ ● ☆ ○ ● ☆ ○

size
colour
shape

d □ ○ □ ○ □ ○ □ ○

position
shape
size

e △ ▷ △ ▷ △ ▷ △

position
shape
size

Creating Patterns

1 Colour an **AAB** pattern. Circle the core of the pattern.

◯ ◯ ◯ ◯ ◯ ◯ ◯ ◯ ◯ ◯ ◯ ◯

2 Colour an **ABC** pattern. Circle the core of the pattern.

◯ ◯ ◯ ◯ ◯ ◯ ◯ ◯ ◯ ◯ ◯ ◯

3 Create a repeating pattern that shows **shape** and **colour** changes.

4 Create a repeating pattern that shows **size** and **colour** changes.

I can create patterns.

Creating Patterns (continued)

5 Colour an **AABB** pattern. Circle the core of the pattern.

◯ ◯ ◯ ◯ ◯ ◯ ◯ ◯ ◯ ◯ ◯

6 Colour an **ABCD** pattern. Circle the core of the pattern.

◯ ◯ ◯ ◯ ◯ ◯ ◯ ◯ ◯ ◯ ◯ ◯

7 Create a growing geometric pattern. Write the pattern rule.

8 Create a shrinking number pattern. Write the pattern rule.

Show What You Know!

1 Circle the core of the repeating pattern.

a ○ ■ ■ ○ ■ ■ ○ ■ ■

b **2 2 3 3 2 2 3 3 2 2 3 3**

2 Extend the pattern by its next two terms.

a 10 100 10 100 10 ____ ____

b △ ● □ △ ● □ △ ____ ____

3 Name the pattern using letters. Circle how the pattern changes.

colour   **shape**   **position**

____   ____   ____   ____   ____   ____

4 Colour an **ABCD** pattern. Circle the core of the pattern.

○ ○ ○ ○ ○ ○ ○ ○ ○ ○ ○ ○

Show What You Know! (continued)

5 Translate the pattern into letters.

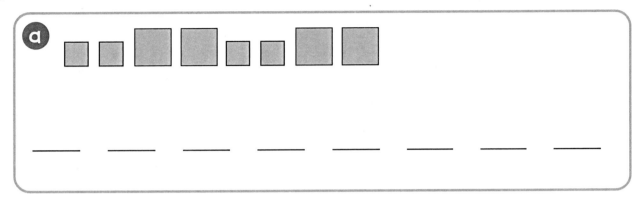

_____   _____   _____   _____   _____   _____   _____   _____

6 Make a growing number pattern.

a **The pattern rule is add 5 each time.**

Start at 25, _____, _____, _____, _____, _____, _____, _____

b **The pattern rule is add 2 each time.**

Start at 100, _____, _____, _____, _____, _____, _____, _____

7 Make a shrinking number pattern.

a **The pattern rule is subtract 10 each time.**

Start at 150, _____, _____, _____, _____, _____, _____, _____

b **The pattern rule is subtract 5 each time.**

Start at 80, _____, _____, _____, _____, _____, _____, _____

I Can Checklist:
Equations & Inequalities

Identify when symbols are being used as variables, and describe how they are being used. For example,

- **I can** recognize that in the equation '3 + □ = 7', the box (□) is a symbol being used as a variable to represent the number 4.
- **I can** identify that in the problem 'if b + 3 = 8, what is b?', the letter 'b' is a variable standing for the number 5.
- **I can** explain that in '5 + y = 10', 'y' is a variable used to represent the number that would make the equation true, which is 5.

Determine what needs to be added to or subtracted from addition and subtraction expressions to make them equivalent. For example,

- **I can** determine that to make 7 + 2 equivalent to 10, I need to add 1 more to the 7 + 2 expression.
- **I can** find out that if I add 1 to 9 in the expression 9 + 3, it becomes equivalent to 11 + 2.
- **I can** decide that to make 20 − 5 the same as 10, I need to subtract 5 more from the 20 − 5 expression.

Identify and use equivalent relationships for whole numbers up to 100, in various contexts. For example,

- **I can** identify that 50 is the same as 45 + 5 in the context of counting coins or scoring in a game.
- **I can** understand that 70 is equivalent to 35 + 35 when measuring the length of two identical objects that are each 35 units long.
- **I can** use the equivalent relationship that 4 groups of 25 are the same as 100 when dividing items into equal groups.

Introducing Variables

A **variable** is a letter or symbol that represents a number we don't know.

 + 5 = 9

This equation means a number we don't know plus 5 equals 9.

We know that 4 + 5 = 9, so = 4!

1 Solve to find the value of the variable.

a

6 + 🍔 = 13

🍔 =

b

5 – 🍎 = 2

🍎 =

c

🧁 + 10 = 20

🧁 =

d

10 – 7 = 📖

📖 =

e

🍩 + 8 = 15

🍩 =

f

20 – 🔔 = 11

🔔 =

2 Write an equation for each problem. Use a letter or symbol to represent the number we don't know. Solve the equation.

a 5 plus a number equals 15.

b A number minus 8 equals 4.

Exploring Variables

A **variable** is a letter or symbol that represents a number we don't know.

$$4 + n = 10$$

This means 4 plus a number we don't know equals 10.

We know that $4 + 6 = 10$, so $n = 6$.

1 Circle the **variable** in the equation.

a
$$6 + n = 13$$

b
$$5 - p = 2$$

c
$$r + 8 = 11$$

d
$$12 - 6 = n$$

e
$$y - 12 = 8$$

f
$$6 + 4 = p$$

2 Circle the equation that matches the word problem.

a Josie has 15 apples. She gives n apples to Gerry. Josie has 12 apples left.

$$15 - n = 12 \qquad n - 15 = 12$$

b Sammy has n cards in his collection. He buys a pack of 10 cards and adds them to the collection. Now Sammy has 25 cards.

$$10 + 25 = n \qquad n + 10 = 25$$

I can identify variables.

Exploring Variables (continued)

3 Evaluate the expression.

a 10 + **n**   when **n** = 7

b **n** – 7   when **n** = 14

c **n** – 9   when **n** = 15

d **n** + 12   when **n** = 6

e 18 – **n**   when **n** = 13

f 16 + **n**   when **n** = 12

4 Use the value of the variables to solve the equations.

n = 5   **k** = 12   **p** = 8

a 5 + **n** = _____

b **p** – 7 = _____

c **k** + 14 = _____

d 16 + **n** = _____

e 19 – **p** = _____

f **k** – 6 = _____

Exploring Addition Sentences

Show three ways to make the number. Use two colours.

1

____ + ____ = 8

____ + ____ = 8

____ + ____ = 8

2

____ + ____ = 4

____ + ____ = 4

____ + ____ = 4

3

____ + ____ = 10

____ + ____ = 10

____ + ____ = 10

4

____ + ____ = 6

____ + ____ = 6

____ + ____ = 6

I can write addition sentences.

Balance It

Draw blocks to make the balance equal on both sides.

1
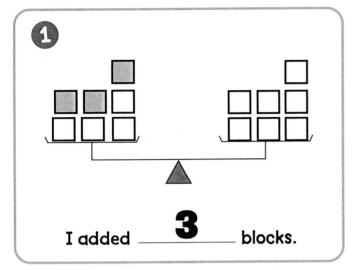

I added __**3**__ blocks.

2
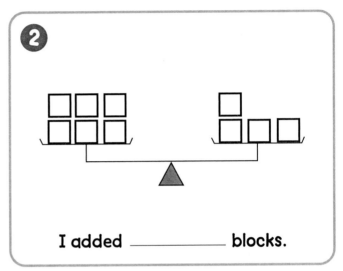

I added _____ blocks.

3
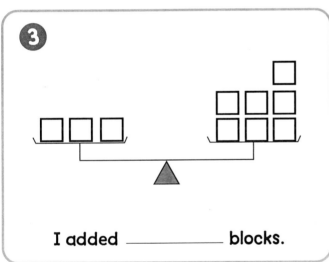

I added _____ blocks.

4
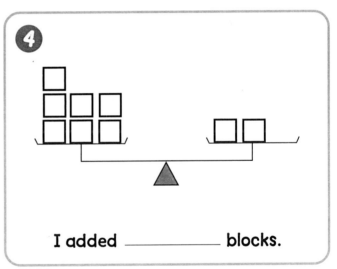

I added _____ blocks.

5
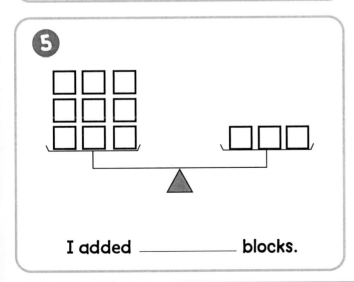

I added _____ blocks.

6
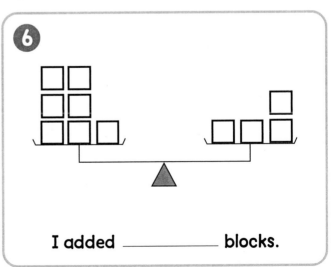

I added _____ blocks.

Making Equal Addition Expressions

A **balanced equation** means both sides of the equal sign equal the same number.

Balanced: **8 + 7 = 15** ✓   Not Balanced: **15 + 9 ≠ 10**

1 Fill in the blank with = or ≠ to make both expressions equal.

a 2 + 9 ⬤ 5 + 6

b 18 + 7 ⬤ 10 + 9

c 12 + 3 ⬤ 8 + 6

2 Fill in the missing numbers to make both number expressions equal.

a (2) + (6) = ⬤ + ⬤

b (4) + (5) = ⬤ + ⬤

c (7) + (8) = ⬤ + ⬤

I can make equal addition expressions.

Finding the Missing Number—Addition

Draw counters to help find the missing number in the equation.

1 $5 + 5 = \boxed{} + 2$

2 $5 + 9 = 7 + \boxed{}$

3 $4 + 8 = 6 + \boxed{}$

4 $2 + 4 = 3 + \boxed{}$

5 $9 + 2 = \boxed{} + 6$

Exploring Subtraction Sentences

Cross out the blocks you want to take away. Colour the blocks left.
Complete the subtraction sentence. Show three different sentences.

1

5 – ___ = ___

5 – ___ = ___

5 – ___ = ___

2

9 – ___ = ___

9 – ___ = ___

9 – ___ = ___

3

6 – ___ = ___

6 – ___ = ___

6 – ___ = ___

4

10 – ___ = ___

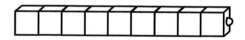

10 – ___ = ___

10 – ___ = ___

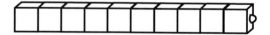

I can write subtraction sentences.

Balance It

Remove blocks to make the balance equal on both sides.

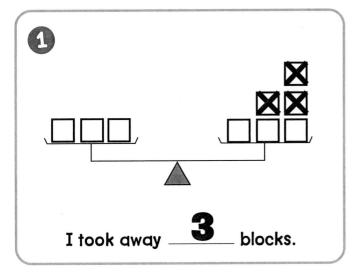

1 I took away ___**3**___ blocks.

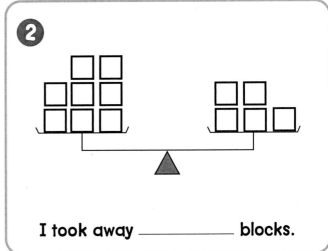

2 I took away _____ blocks.

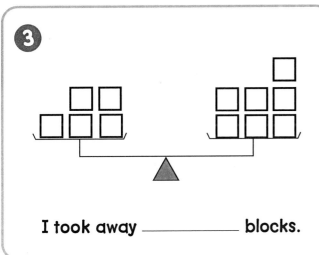

3 I took away _____ blocks.

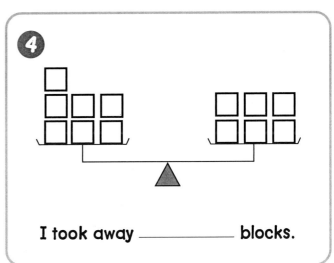

4 I took away _____ blocks.

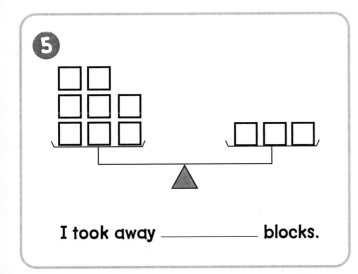

5 I took away _____ blocks.

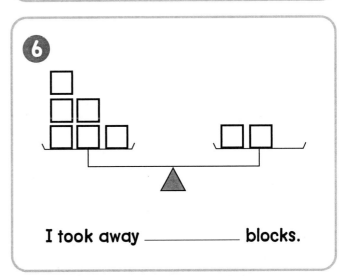

6 I took away _____ blocks.

Making Equal Subtraction Expressions

A **balanced equation** means both sides of the equal sign equal the same number.

Balanced: **8 - 7 = 1** ✓   Not Balanced: **15 - 9 ≠ 10**

1 Are the expressions equal? Fill in the blank with = or ≠.

a **9 - 2** ◯ **5 - 6**

b **18 - 7** ◯ **20 - 9**

c **12 - 3** ◯ **8 - 6**

2 Fill in the missing numbers to make both expressions equal.

a   -   = ◯ - ◯

b ⑮ - ⑨ = ◯ - ◯

c ⑨ - ⑦ = ◯ - ◯

✓ **I can make equal subtraction expressions.**

Finding the Missing Number—Subtraction

Draw counters to help find the missing number in the equation.

1 $17 - 8 = 10 -$ ⬭

2 $13 - 7 = 11 -$ ⬭

3 $12 - 6 = 10 -$ ⬭

4 $15 - 10 = 8 -$ ⬭

5 $11 - 4 = 10 -$ ⬭

Show What You Know!

1 Solve to find the value of the variable.

a

10 + 🍎 = 18

🍎 =

b

12 − 🍔 = 4

🍔 =

c

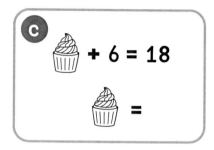 + 6 = 18

🧁 =

2 Use the value of the variables to solve the equation.

$n = 10$ $r = 8$ $k = 15$

a $6 + n =$ _____

b $k - 10 =$ _____

c $r - 3 =$ _____

d $12 + r =$ _____

3 Show two ways to make each number. Use two colours.

a

_____ + _____ = 8

_____ + _____ = 8

b

5 − ____ = ____

5 − ____ = ____

Show What You Know! (continued)

4 Add or remove blocks to make the balance equal on both sides.

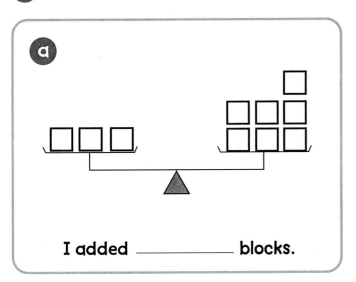

a

I added _____ blocks.

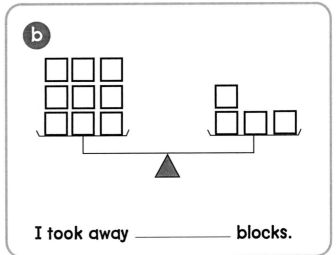

b

I took away _____ blocks.

5 Are the expressions equal? Fill in the blank with **=** or **≠**.

6 + 3 ◯ 4 + 7

6 Fill in the missing numbers to make both expressions equal.

(8) - (4) = ◯ - ◯

7 Draw counters to help find the missing number in the equation.

12 + 6 = ⬭ + 7

I Can Checklist:
Coding Skills

Solve problems and create computational representations of mathematical situations by writing and executing code, including code that involves sequential and concurrent events. For example,

- *I can use coding to solve math problems or create representations of math situations.*

- *I can write code to count how many apples are in a basket or to show a number line on the computer screen.*

- *I can make things happen in a specific order, like having the computer show the numbers from 1 to 10, one by one.*

Read and alter existing code, including code that involves sequential and concurrent events, and describe how changes to the code affect the outcomes. For example,

- *I can look at code that someone else wrote and understand what it does.*

- *I can make changes to the code, like changing the numbers or the order of events, and see how it affects the outcome.*

- *I can explain what will happen differently when I make changes to the code.*

Coding in Everyday Life!

Coding is like giving the computer a set of instructions in a language it understands, one step at a time.

For example, these things need coding to run:

washing machine   **television**   **cell phone**

1 Colour the pictures of things that need coding to run.

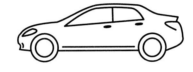

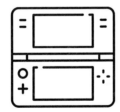

2 List some electronics that people use that need coding to run.

1 _____

2 _____

3 _____

Reading Code

Code: the language we use to give a computer step-by-step instructions or commands.

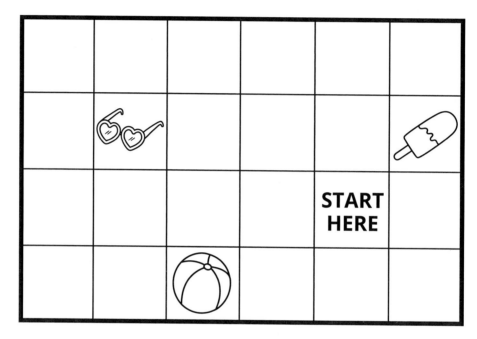

Begin on the "Start Here" square.
Follow the code and circle the object you land on.

1 ↑ ↑ ← ← ← ↓

2 ← ↓ → → ↑ ↑

I can read code.

Writing Code

1. Complete the line of code by drawing the commands using arrows.

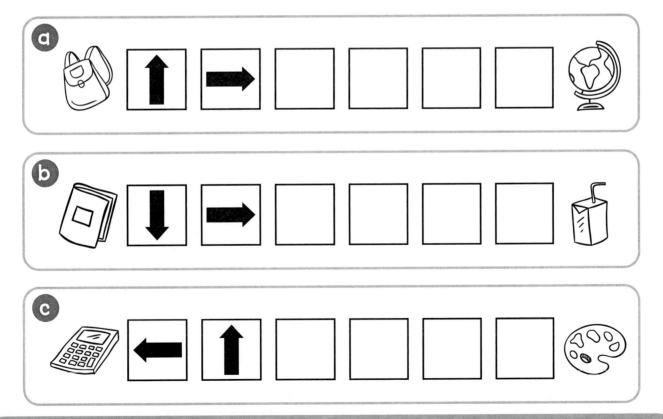

Writing Code (continued)

								3
	1							
					2			
			5					
							4	

2 Draw arrows on the lines to show the path to get from 1 to 5.

1 _____ 2

2 _____ 3

3 _____ 4

4 _____ 5

I can write code.

Concurrent Code

Concurrent codes are events that happen at the same time.

For example,

Bear and Raccoon are racing to get to the apple!

Bear gets to the apple in 4 spaces.

Raccoon gets to the apple in 5 spaces.

Bear gets to the apple first.

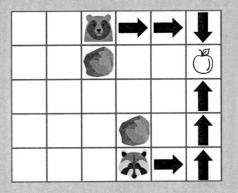

Use two different colours to draw the path Pig and Mouse take to get to the apple. Make sure they avoid the rocks!

1 How many spaces did it take Pig to get to the apple? _____

2 How many spaces did it take Mouse to get to the apple? _____

3 Who got to the apple first? _____

Altering Code

The word *alter* means to change.

Alter the code means to write the same code in a different way or order.

X	N	S	V	N	L	Z	Q
🏀	B	E	Z	I	A	R	B
S	R	A	C	H	Y	T	🏰

1 From the 🏀 square, follow the code below to spell the secret word.

➡ ➡ ⬇ ➡ ➡

a What word did the code spell? _____

b Use the line below to alter the code above to spell the word "bears".

_____

2 From the 🏰 square, the following code spells the word "train."

⬅ ⬆ ⬅ ⬅ ⬆

Use the line below to alter the code above to spell the word "brain."

_____

✓ I can alter code.

Altering Code (continued)

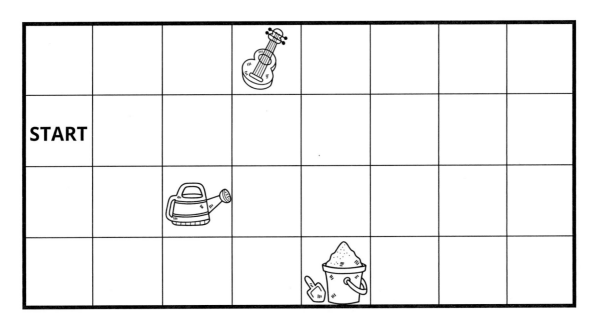

3 From the "Start" square, follow the arrows to get to an object. On the line, draw arrows to show a different way you can get to the same object.

a Get to the 🎸. ➡ ➡ ➡ ⬆

_____

b Get to the 🪣. ⬇ ➡ ➡

_____

c Get to the 🪣. ➡ ⬇ ⬇ ➡ ➡ ➡

_____

Show What You Know!

1 Begin on the "Start Here" square.
Follow the code and circle the object you land on.

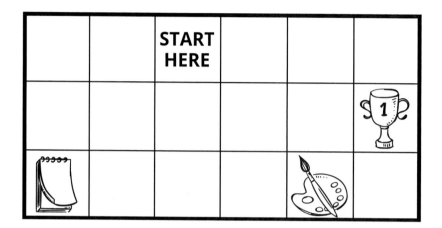

2 Complete the line of code by drawing the commands using arrows.

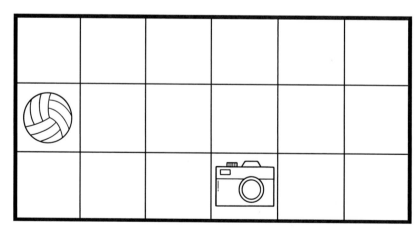

Show What You Know! (continued)

3 Use two different colours to draw the path Bear and Mouse take to get to the apple. Make sure they avoid the rocks!

Circle the animal that gets to the apple in fewer steps.

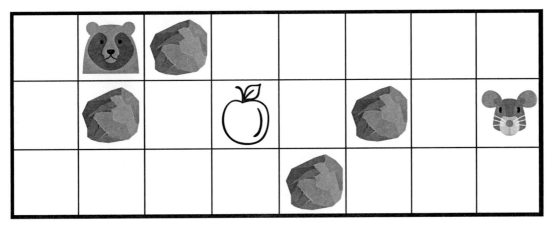

4 From the "Start" square, follow the arrows to get to the butterfly. On the line, draw arrows to show a different way you can get to the butterfly.

Get to the 🦋. ↓ → → ↑ ↑ → →

I Can Checklist:
Financial Literacy

Identify different ways of representing the same amount of money up to Canadian 200¢ using various combinations of coins, and up to $200 using various combinations of $1 and $2 coins and $5, $10, $20, $50, and $100 bills. For example,

- *I can* represent 50¢ using patterning:
  10 nickels
  8 nickels and 1 dime
  6 nickels and 2 dimes
  4 nickels and 3 dimes
  2 nickels and 4 dimes
  5 dimes

- *I can* represent 50¢ with the least number of coins.

- *I can* represent 50¢ with the greatest number of coins.

- *I can* represent $2 in different ways:
  8 quarters
  2 loonies

- *I can* decompose $100 in various ways
  2 fifty dollar bills
  5 twenty dollar bills

Getting to Know Coins

Draw a line from the coin to its value.
Then match the coin to its name.

100 cents  toonie

10 cents  loonie

5 cents nickel

200 cents  dime

25 cents  quarter

Exploring Canadian Bills

This is a 5 dollar bill.

This bill is worth $5 or 5 dollars.

It has Sir Wilfrid Laurier on one side.

Colour the bill blue.

This is a 10 dollar bill.

This bill is worth $10 or 10 dollars.

It has Viola Desmond on one side.

Colour the bill purple.

This is a 20 dollar bill.

This bill is worth $20 or 20 dollars.

It has Queen Elizabeth II on one side.

Colour the bill green.

Exploring Canadian Bills (continued)

This is a 50 dollar bill.

This bill is worth $50 or 50 dollars.

It has William Lyon Mackenzie King on one side.

Colour the bill ⟨ red ⟩.

This is a 100 dollar bill.

This bill is worth $100 or 100 dollars.

It has Sir Robert Borden on one side.

Colour the bill ⟨ brown ⟩.

Counting Coins

Count the coins in both sets. Circle the coins that add up to the price tag.

1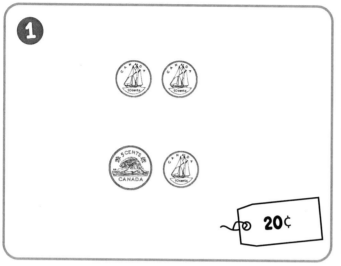

2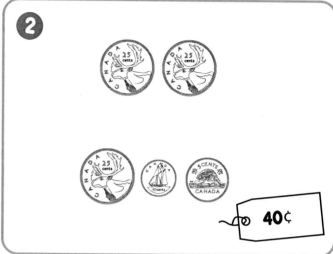

3

4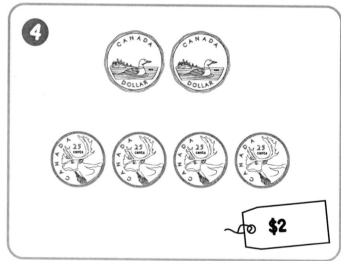

5

6

I can count coins.

Show Two Different Ways
to Make the Same Amount

Show two different ways to make the same amount. Draw the coins.

First Way	Second Way
1 20¢	
2 75¢	
3 $1.85	
4 $2.00	

Counting Canadian Bills

Count the money in the set.
Draw a line from the set of money to the correct price tag.

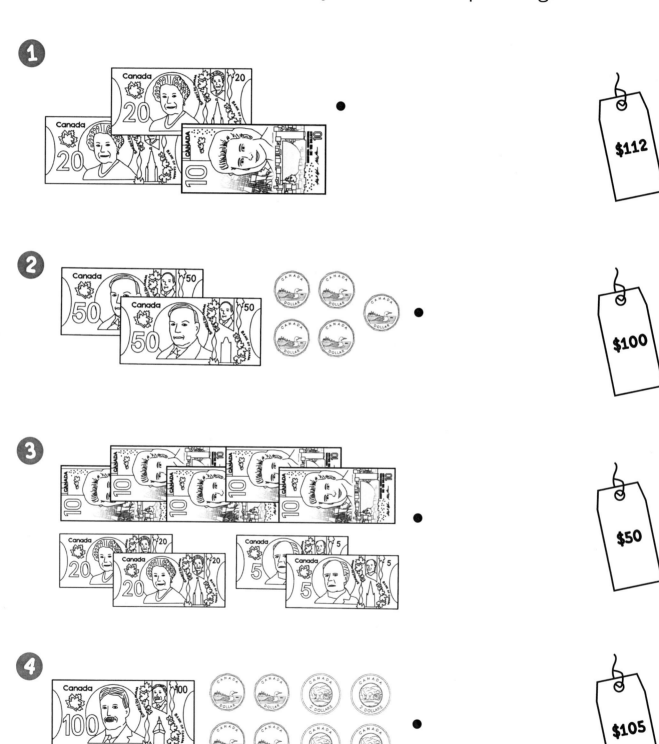

1 • $112

2 • $100

3 • $50

4 • $105

I can count money amounts.

Comparing Money Amounts

Compare the bills. Print the correct symbol in the box.

greater than   less than   equal to

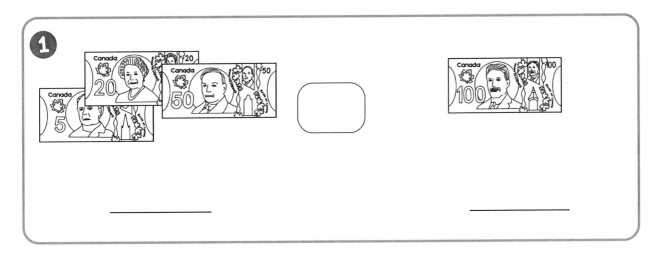

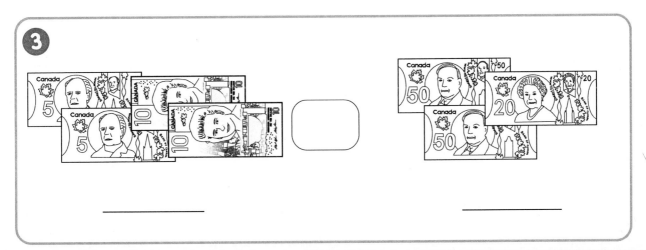

Showing Bill Amounts in Different Ways

Show two ways of making the same money amount with different bills.

First Way	Second Way
1 $50	
2 $100	
3 $25	
4 $200	

I can show bill amounts in different ways. © Chalkboard Publishing Inc

Buying Sports Equipment

Bike

Baseball and bat

Ice skates

Soccer ball

$200 $40 $85 $15

1 What is the price of a soccer ball and a baseball and bat?

2 What is the price of ice skates and a baseball and bat?

3 You have $200 to buy new sports equipment.
What will you choose? Will you get change back?

Show What You Know!

1 Count the coins in each set. Circle the coins that add up to the price tag.

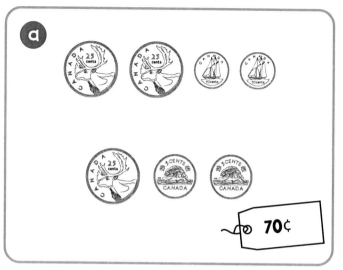

70¢

$1.25

2 Show two different ways to make the same amount.
Draw the coins or bills.

First Way	Second Way

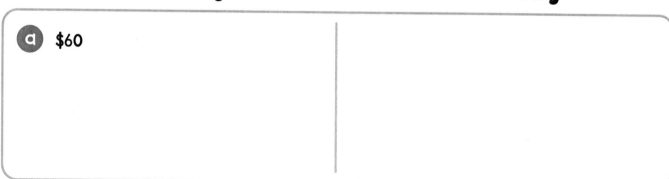

a $60

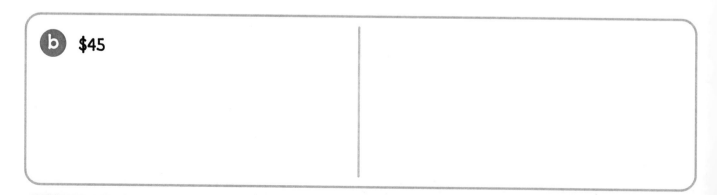

b $45

Show What You Know! (continued)

3 Compare the bills. Print the correct symbol in the box.

greater than **less than** **equal to**

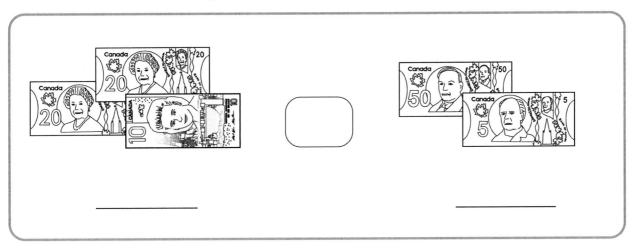

_____   _____

4 Count the money in the set.
Draw a line from the set of money to the correct price tag.

a

b

c

$15

$26

$84

I Can Checklist:
Data Literacy

Sort sets of data about people or things according to two attributes, using tables and logic diagrams, including Venn and Carroll diagrams. For example,

- *I can sort a collection of my favourite toys into a Venn diagram based on their colour and type.*

- *I can use a Carroll diagram to sort my classmates according to their hair colour and whether they wear glasses or not.*

Collect data through observations, experiments, or interviews to answer questions of interest that focus on two pieces of information, and organize the data in two-way tally tables. For example,

- *I can interview my classmates about their favourite fruit and colour, then organize the data in a two-way tally table.*

Display sets of data, using one-to-one correspondence, in concrete graphs, pictographs, line plots, and bar graphs with proper sources, titles, and labels. For example,

- *I can create different graphs to display the number of different types of pets my classmates have.*

Identify the mode(s), if any, for various data sets presented in concrete graphs, pictographs, line plots, bar graphs, and tables, and explain what this measure indicates about the data. For example,

- *I can identify the most common score on our class math test (the mode) from a list of all the scores and explain what this means.*

Analyze different sets of data presented in various ways, including in logic diagrams, line plots, and bar graphs, by asking and answering questions about the data and drawing conclusions, then make convincing arguments and informed decisions. For example,

- *I can look at a bar graph of the number of books each student read this month, ask questions about who read the most, who read the least, and use this information to set a reading goal for next month.*

Create Your Own Survey!

What is your favourite _____?

- pet
- colour
- fruit
- home activity
- snack
- season
- winter activity
- summer activity
- sport
- recess activity

- pizza topping
- ice cream flavour
- dessert
- restaurant
- meal
- day of the week
- superhero
- author
- reading genre
- music genre

- school subject
- holiday
- cereal
- breakfast meal
- game
- coin
- cartoon
- lunch meal
- vegetable
- time of day

Make your own questions...

- What do you prefer?
- What do you like best?

- What is your estimation?
- What is your prediction?

More ideas:

- How many people are in your family?
- What colour hair do you have?
- What colour eyes do you have?
- Would you rather live in the rainforest or the ocean?

Exploring Venn Diagrams

A **Venn diagram** is a way to sort data into two or three circles that overlap in the middle.

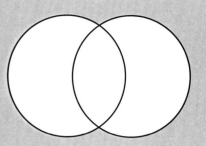

Each side shows the people who like one of two different activities. People who are in the middle where the circles overlap like both activities.

Favourite Playground Activity

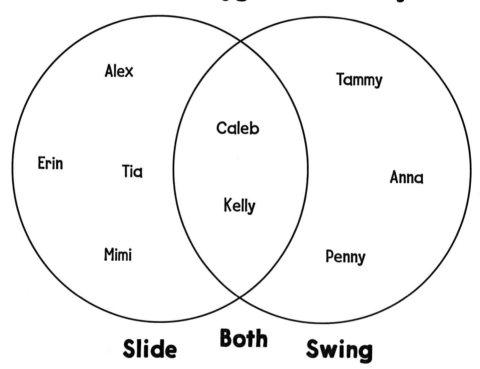

Alex

Tammy

Caleb

Erin   Tia

Anna

Kelly

Mimi

Penny

Slide   **Both**   **Swing**

Which children like to play on the **Swing**, but not on the **Slide**?

_____

✓ I can read Venn diagrams.

Sorting into a Venn Diagram

Sort the jersey numbers into the correct category.

Team Jersey Numbers

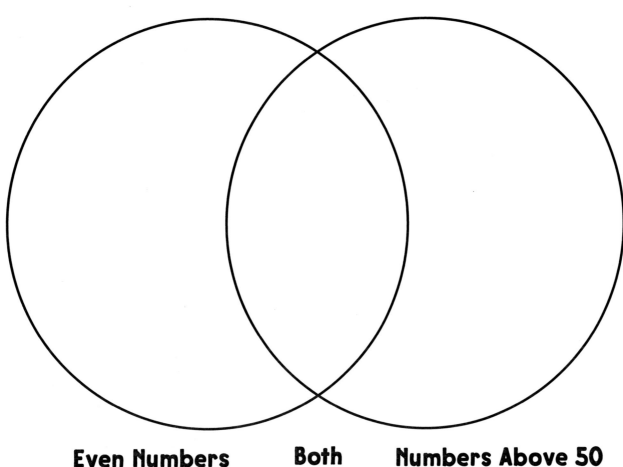

Even Numbers   **Both**   **Numbers Above 50**

Sorting into a Carroll Diagram

1 Sort the clothing into the correct category.

tank top   snow pants   parka   T-shirt

sweatshirt   sweater   shorts   pants

	Tops	Bottoms
Summer Clothing		
Winter Clothing		

I can sort using a Carroll diagram.

Sorting into a Carroll Diagram (continued)

2 Look at the animals.
Write the name of the animals into the correct categories.

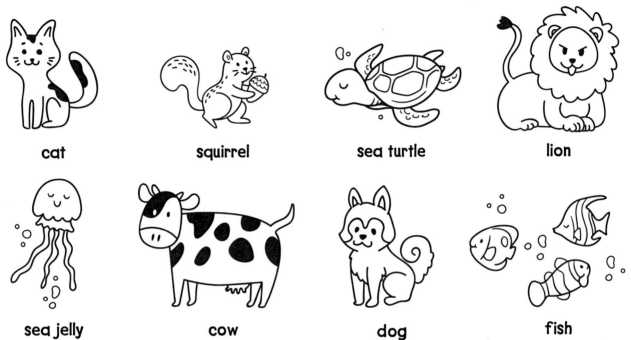

| cat | squirrel | sea turtle | lion |

| sea jelly | cow | dog | fish |

	Lives on Land	**Lives Underwater**
Is Often a Household Pet		
Is Not a Household Pet		

Exploring Tally Charts

Each **tally mark** represents 1.

A tally chart counts data in groups of **5**.

||||| = 5

1 Answer the questions for the tally chart.

Favourite Colour Tally

Colour	Tally	Number
yellow	||||| |||||	
blue	|||||	
purple	|||	

a What was the most popular colour?

_____

b What was the least popular colour?

_____

c How many in total chose blue or yellow?

_____

I can read tally charts.

Exploring Tally Charts (continued)

2) Answer the questions for the tally chart.

Favourite Animal Tally

Animal	Tally	Number
dog	‖‖‖‖ ‖‖‖‖	
cat	‖‖‖‖ ‖‖‖	
bird	‖‖‖‖	

a) What was the most popular animal?

_____

b) What was the least popular animal?

_____

c) How many in total chose dogs or cats?

_____

d) How many more people chose cats over birds?

_____

Exploring Pictographs

A **pictograph** is a way to show data using pictures.

1 Read the pictograph to answer the questions.

Favourite Sports

Type of Sport	
Football	☺ ☺
Baseball	☺ ☺ ☺
Hockey	☺ ☺ ☺ ☺

☺ equals **2** votes

Number of Votes

a What was the most popular sport?

_____

b What was the least popular sport?

_____

c How many voted for hockey?

_____

I can read pictographs.

Exploring Pictographs (continued)

2 Read the pictograph to answer the questions.

Apple Picking

Student	Number of Apples Picked
Liam	🍎 🍎 🍎
Anita	🍎
Bailey	🍎 🍎 🍎 🍎

🍎 equals 5 apples picked

Number of Apples Picked

a How many apples picked does one apple symbol represent?

_____

b Who picked the most apples?

_____

c Who picked the least apples?

_____

d How many more apples did Bailey pick than Liam?

_____

Exploring Bar Graphs

A **bar graph** is a way to show data and compare information. The bars can go up or across the graph.

1 Read the bar graph to answer the questions.

Favourite Toys

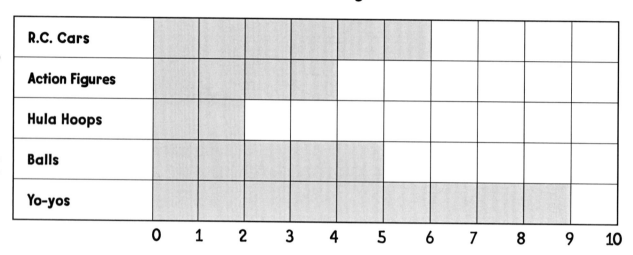

Type of Toy	Number of Votes
R.C. Cars	6
Action Figures	3
Hula Hoops	1
Balls	5
Yo-yos	9

a What was the most popular toy?

_____

b What was the least popular toy?

_____

c How many fewer children like hula hoops than R.C cars?

_____

I can read bar graphs.

Exploring Bar Graphs (continued)

2 Read the bar graph to answer the questions.

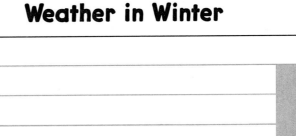

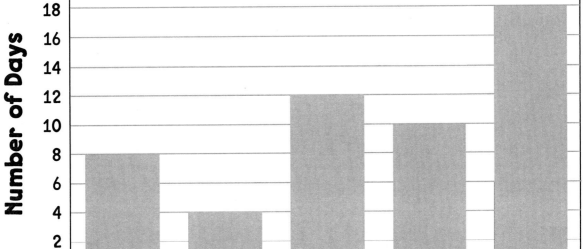

a What was the most common type of weather?

_____

b How many windy days were there?

_____

c How many more sunny days were there than cloudy days?

_____

Exploring Line Plots

A **line plot** shows a mark above a number for each value in a data set.

Two students voted that they have one sibling.

Number of Siblings

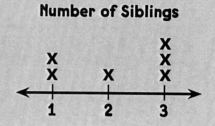

1 Read the line plot to answer the questions.

Number of Books Read

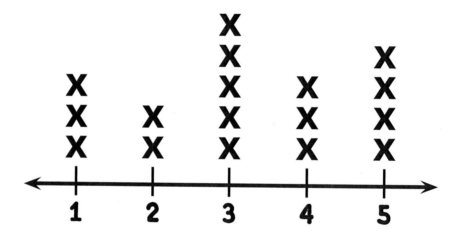

a How many students read 5 books?

_____

b What was the most common number of books read?

_____

c Which number of books were read the same amount?

_____

I can read line plots.

Exploring Line Plots (continued)

2 Use the chart below to complete the line plot and answer the questions.

Number of Pets	1	2	3	4	5	6
Student Votes	5	8	2	3	2	1

Number of Pets

1   2   3   4   5   6

a How many students have 5 pets?

_____

b What was the most common number of pets owned?

_____

c Which number of pets owned was voted for 3 times?

_____

Finding the Mode

The **mode** is the number that appears the most often in a data set.

1 Read the tally chart and find the mode.

a

Drink	Tally	Number
apple juice	ⅢⅡ ⅢⅡ	10
orange juice	ⅢⅡ ⅢⅡ	10
2% milk	|||	3
soda pop	||	2

The mode is...

_____

b

Colour	Tally	Number
red	||||	4
blue	ⅢⅡ |||	8
green	ⅢⅡ |||	8
purple	ⅢⅡ ||	7

The mode is...

_____

I can find the mode.

Finding the Mode (continued)

2 Group the numbers to find the mode.

a 5, 10, 6, 5

Mode: _____

b 25, 100, 50, 100, 20

Mode: _____

c 1, 4, 4, 6, 9, 4, 7

Mode: _____

d 12, 3, 9, 3, 3, 9, 10

Mode: _____

e 7, 15, 20, 20, 20, 7

Mode: _____

f 19, 30, 9, 1, 1, 17, 1

Mode: _____

Representing Data in Different Ways

1 Complete the tally chart and bar graph.

Favourite Pets Chart

Pet	Tally	Number
Dog		4
Cat		8
Hamster		1
Bird		5

Favourite Pets Graph

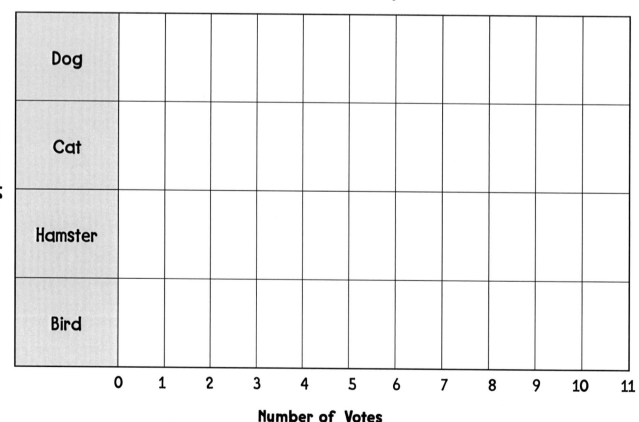

Type of Pet

Dog

Cat

Hamster

Bird

0 1 2 3 4 5 6 7 8 9 10 11

Number of Votes

I can represent data in different ways.

Representing Data in Different Ways (continued)

2 Look at the tally chart and bar graph and answer the questions.

a What was the most popular pet?

_____

b What was the least popular pet?

_____

c How many people in total chose either a dog or a bird?

_____

d How many more people chose a cat than a hamster?

_____

e How many people chose a hamster?

_____

Show What You Know!

1 Complete the tally chart and bar graph.

Favourite Sport Chart

Sport	Tally	Number
Soccer ⚽		6
Hockey 🏒		10
Basketball 🏀		3
Baseball ⚾		5

Favourite Sport Graph

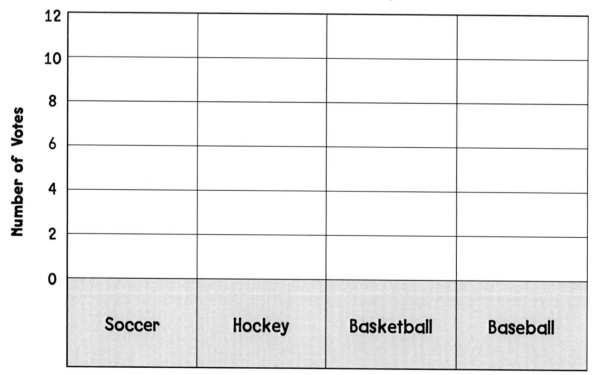

Show What You Know! (continued)

2 Read the pictograph to answer the questions.

Fruit Sales

Number of Fruits Sold

equals **2** fruits sold

a How many fruits sold does one star symbol represent?

_____

b How many cherries were sold?

_____

3 Group the numbers to find the mode.

a 50, 50, 25, 5, 15, 50

Mode: _____

b 10, 30, 4, 5, 4, 15

Mode: _____

I Can Checklist:
Probability

Use mathematical language, including the terms "impossible," "possible," and "certain," to describe the likelihood of complementary events happening, and use that likelihood to make predictions and informed decisions. For example,

- *I can* use the term "impossible" to describe the likelihood of finding a dinosaur in my backyard.

- *I can* use the term "possible" when discussing the chance of it raining tomorrow, based on the weather forecast.

- *I can* say it's "certain" that there are 7 days in a week, and use this to plan my schedule.

Make and test predictions about the likelihood that the mode(s) of a data set from one population will be the same for data collected from a different population. For example,

- *I can* make a prediction that the most common pet (the mode) in my class will also be the most common pet in another second-grade class, and I can test this by conducting a survey.

- *I can* predict that the most liked ice cream flavour in my family will also be the most liked flavour in my neighbourhood, and test this prediction by asking around.

- *I can* predict that the most common car colour in my town will also be the most common car colour in a nearby town, and I can test this by counting car colours in both towns.

Exploring Probability

Probability is the chance of something happening.

If something is sure to happen, like the sun rising tomorrow, it has a high probability.

If something is unlikely, like seeing a living dinosaur, it has a low probability.

It's a way to guess what might happen based on what we know.

Circle the probability of the event happening.

1  What is the probability of finding a white seashell during a trip to the beach?

certain   **possible**   **impossible**

2 What is the probability of finding a real-life mermaid in a swimming pool?

certain   **possible**   **impossible**

3 What is the probability of the sun rising tomorrow?

certain   **possible**   **impossible**

4  What is the probability of hearing a dog bark while you are outside?

certain   **possible**   **impossible**

What Is the Probability?

1 Circle the probability for the question.

 What is the probability of getting a ● ?

likely   unlikely   certain   impossible

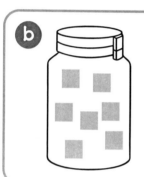 What is the probability of getting a ● ?

likely   unlikely   certain   impossible

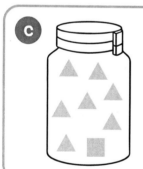 What is the probability of getting a ■ ?

likely   unlikely   certain   impossible

 What is the probability of getting a ★ ?

likely   unlikely   certain   impossible

I can understand probability.

What Is the Probability? (continued)

2 You are at the park. Think of an event happening for each likelihood.

a Certain:

_____

b Possible:

_____

c Impossible:

_____

3 You are at the zoo. Think of an event happening for each likelihood.

a Certain:

_____

b Possible:

_____

c Impossible:

_____

Thinking About Likelihood

1 Circle if the event is **likely** or **unlikely** to occur.

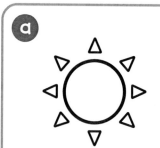 **a** The weather in July was hot and sunny. What is the probability of it being the same weather in December?

likely   unlikely

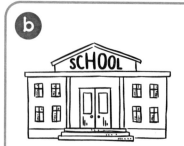 **b** School started at 8 a.m. today. What is the probability of school starting at the same time tomorrow?

likely   unlikely

 **c** It was dark when I went to bed today.
What is the probability of it being dark when I go to bed tomorrow?

likely   unlikely

 **d** The Grade 2 class has homework after school. What is the probability of the parents of the Grade 2 class having homework?

likely   unlikely

I can understand likelihood.

Thinking About Likelihood (continued)

2 The Grade 2 class was surveyed about their favourite pizza toppings. Look at the results and answer the questions.

Favourite Pizza Topping Tally

Pizza Topping	Tally	Number
pepperoni	|||| ||||	
cheese	|||| ||||	
mushrooms	|||	
onions	|||	

a What is the mode of the data set?

_____

b If another Grade 2 class is surveyed, is it likely or unlikely that the results will be the same? Explain your reasoning.

_____

_____

_____

Show What You Know!

1 Circle the probability of the event happening.

a What is the probability of an ice cube melting when left in the sun?

certain   **possible**   **impossible**

b What is the probability of a tree walking and moving from one place to another?

certain   **possible**   **impossible**

2 Circle the probability for the question.

a What is the probability of getting a 🔵 ?

likely   **unlikely**   **certain**   **impossible**

b What is the probability of getting a ⬜ ?

likely   **unlikely**   **certain**   **impossible**

Show What You Know! (continued)

3 You are at the beach. Think of an event happening for each likelihood.

a Certain:

_____

b Possible:

_____

c Impossible:

_____

4 The Grade 2 class was surveyed about their favourite movie genre. Look at the results and answer the questions.

Genre	Comedy	Action	Adventure	Thriller
Student Votes	8	6	5	8

a What is the mode of the data set?

_____

b If another Grade 2 class is surveyed, is it likely or unlikely that the results will be the same?

likely   **unlikely**

I Can Checklist:
Geometric & Spatial Reasoning

Sort and identify two-dimensional shapes by comparing number of sides, side lengths, angles, and number of lines of symmetry. For example,

- *I can sort a collection of shapes by the number of sides each one has.*
- *I can find the lines of symmetry in a regular hexagon.*

Compose and decompose two-dimensional shapes, and show that the area of a shape remains constant regardless of how its parts are rearranged. For example,

- *I can break a rectangle into smaller squares or rectangles and rearrange them to form the same rectangle.*
- *I can combine different triangles to create a square, showing that the total area remains the same.*

Identify congruent lengths and angles in two-dimensional shapes by mentally and physically matching them, and determine if the shapes are congruent. For example,

- *I can identify two shapes as congruent when I overlay one on the other and they match perfectly.*

Location & Movement

Create and interpret simple maps of familiar places. For example,

- *I can create a simple map of my bedroom, indicating where my bed, desk, and bookshelf are located.*
- *I can interpret a map of my school, pointing out where the classroom, playground, and cafeteria are.*

Describe the relative positions of several objects and the movements needed to get from one object to another. For example,

- *I can describe how to get from my desk to the classroom door: "Turn left at the bookshelf, then walk straight until you reach the door."*

Identifying 2D Shapes

Colour the shapes using the colour key.

Colour the circles.	green	Colour the triangles.	red
Colour the squares.	orange	Colour the pentagons.	purple
Colour the rectangles.	blue	Colour the octagons.	yellow

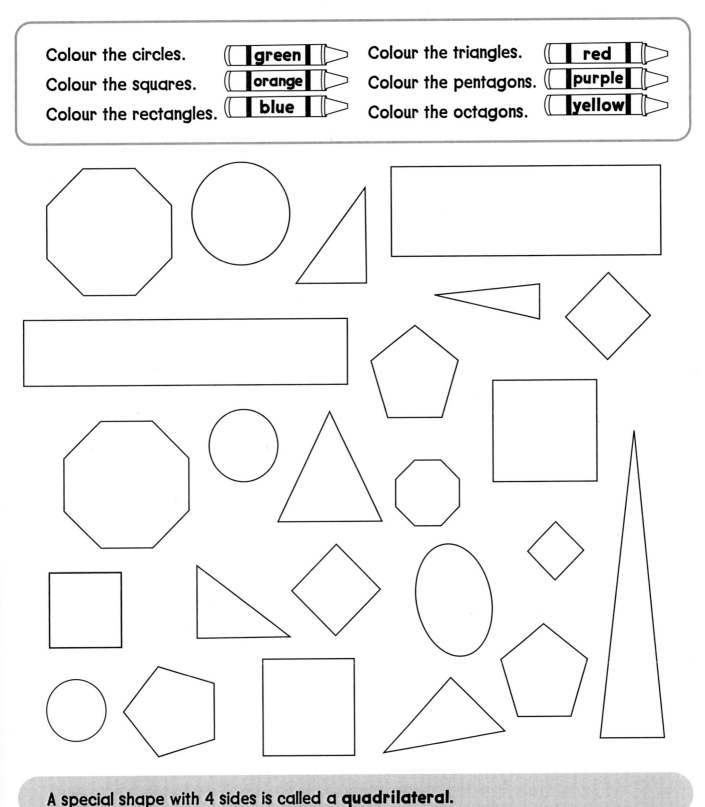

A special shape with 4 sides is called a **quadrilateral.**

Exploring Polygons

A **polygon** is a 2D shape with three or more sides.

A corner of a polygon is a **vertex**. The plural of vertex is **vertices**.

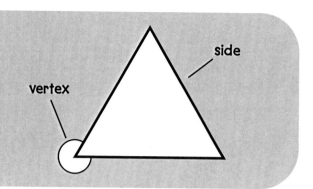

Fill in the chart.

Shape	Trace the Shape	Number of Sides	Number of Vertices

I can identify polygons.

Geometry and Spatial Sense

1 Colour the shapes with less than 5 sides.

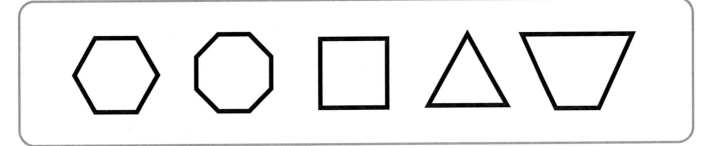

2 Colour the shapes with 3 sides.

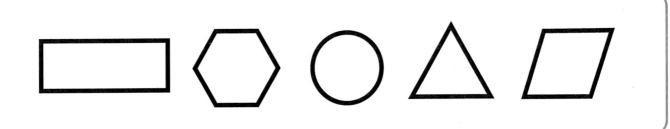

3 Colour the shapes with more than 4 vertices.

4 Colour the shapes with less than 5 vertices.

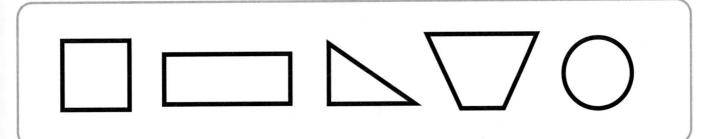

Exploring Symmetry

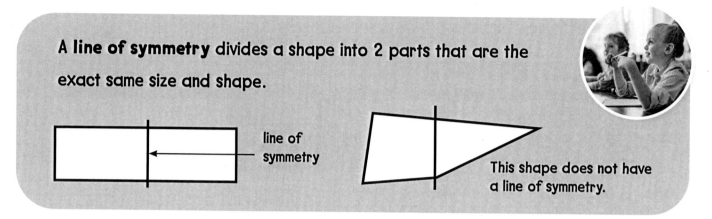

A **line of symmetry** divides a shape into 2 parts that are the exact same size and shape.

line of symmetry

This shape does not have a line of symmetry.

The shape has a dotted line through it. Is the dotted line a line of symmetry? Circle **YES** or **NO**.

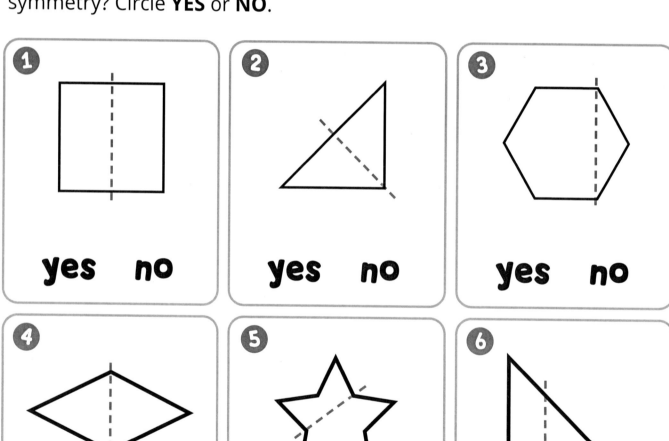

1

yes   no

2

yes   no

3

yes   no

4

yes   no

5

yes   no

6

yes   no

I can identify symmetry.

Decomposing Shapes

Circle the shapes that can be decomposed from each shape.

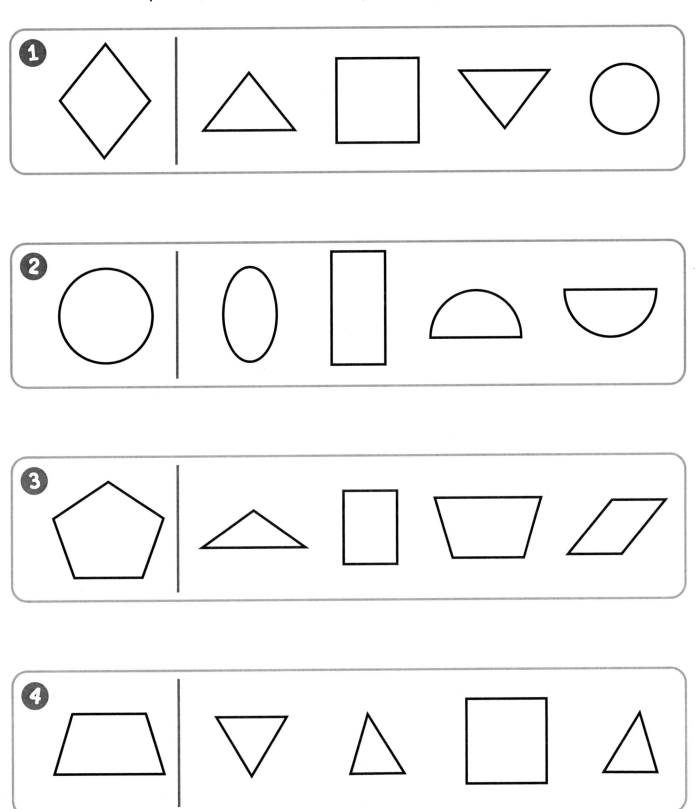

3D Figures

Draw a line from the correct 3D figure to the object. Think about how these everday objects and three-dimensional figures are similar or different. Explain your thinking to a friend.

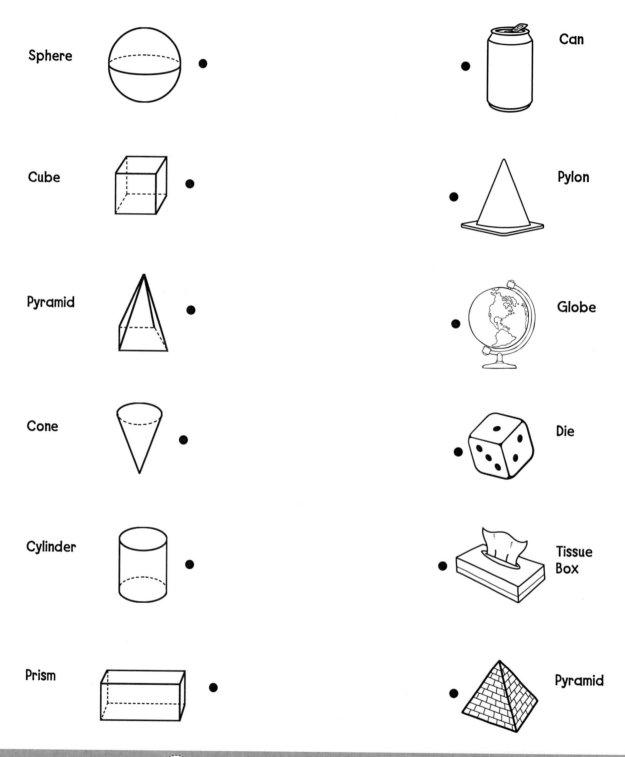

Sphere

Cube

Pyramid

Cone

Cylinder

Prism

Can

Pylon

Globe

Die

Tissue Box

Pyramid

I can identify 3D figures.

Sorting 3D Figures

1 Circle the 3D figures that **can roll**.

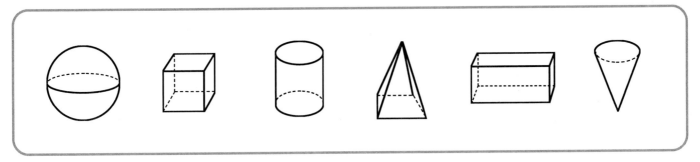

2 Circle the 3D figures that **cannot roll**.

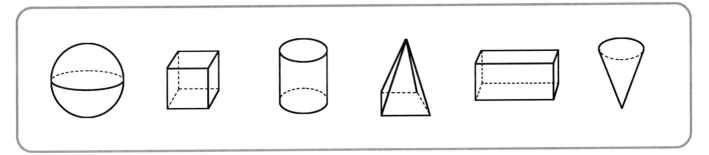

3 Circle the 3D figures that **cannot stack** on each other.

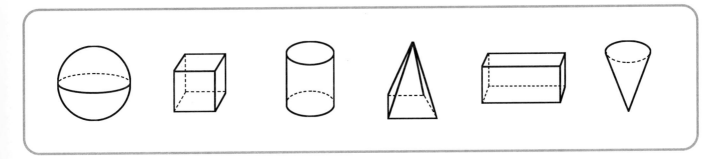

4 Circle the name of the 3D object that you can make from the pieces.

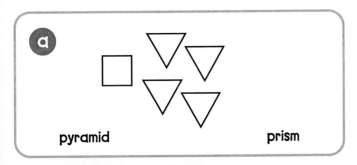

a

pyramid   prism

b

pyramid   cube

Congruent Shapes

Congruent shapes are exactly the same size and shape.

✔ ◢◣   ✘ ◢◣

Colour the shapes that are congruent ⬅ green ▷.
Colour the shapes that are not congruent ⬅ blue ▷.

1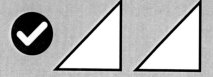

2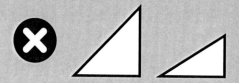

3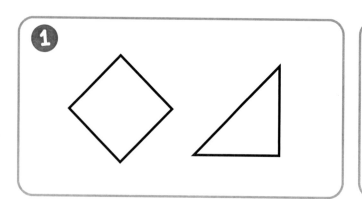

4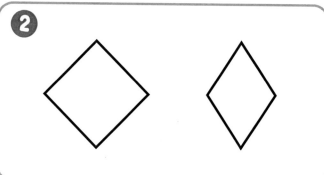

5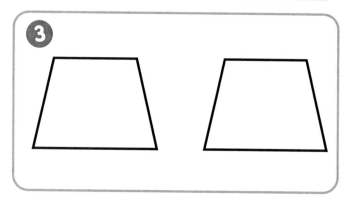

6

I can identify congruent shapes.   © Chalkboard Publishing Inc

Positional Words

Draw a line from the dog to the correct positional word.

 •

• **behind**

 •

• **between**

 •

• **in front of**

 •

• **above**

 •

• **inside**

Reading a Map

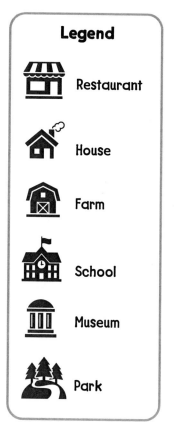

Legend

Restaurant

House

Farm

School

Museum

Park

1 How many houses are there? _____

2 How many restaurants are there? _____

3 What building is next to the school? _____

4 What building is above the park? _____

5 What is near the farm? _____

I can read a map.

Location and Movement

Follow the instructions.

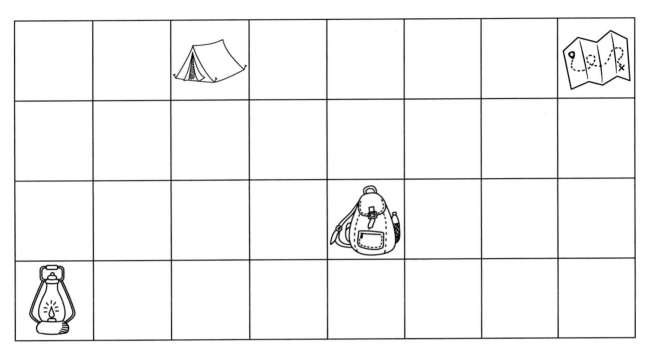

1 Draw a ◯ 1 space left and 2 spaces down from the .

2 Draw a △ 3 spaces right and 1 space down from the .

3 Describe the direction and number of spaces to get from the to the .

_____

4 Describe the direction and number of spaces to get from the to the .

_____

Show What You Know!

1 Colour the shapes using the colour key.

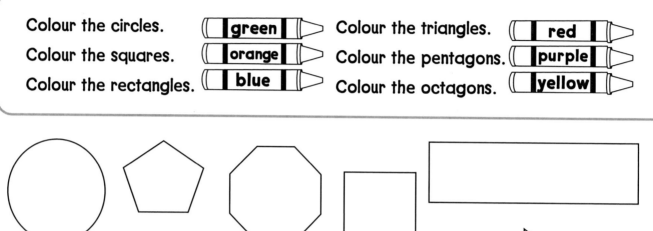

Colour the circles. **green** Colour the triangles. **red**
Colour the squares. **orange** Colour the pentagons. **purple**
Colour the rectangles. **blue** Colour the octagons. **yellow**

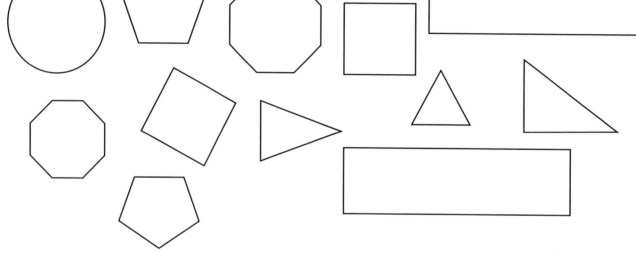

2 The shape has a dotted line through it. Is the dotted line a line of symmetry? Circle **YES** or **NO**.

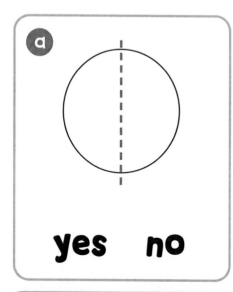

a yes   no

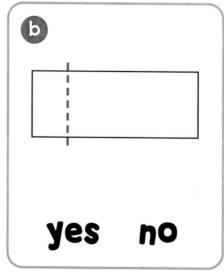

b yes   no

c yes   no

Show What You Know! (continued)

3 Colour the shapes that are congruent (green) .
Colour the shapes that are not congruent (blue) .

a
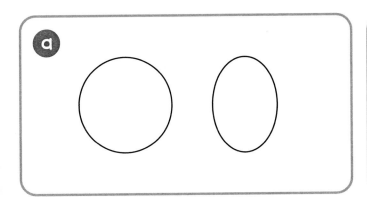

b
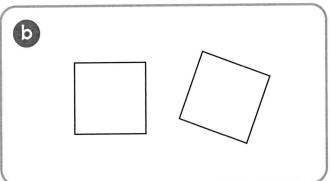

4 Follow the instructions.

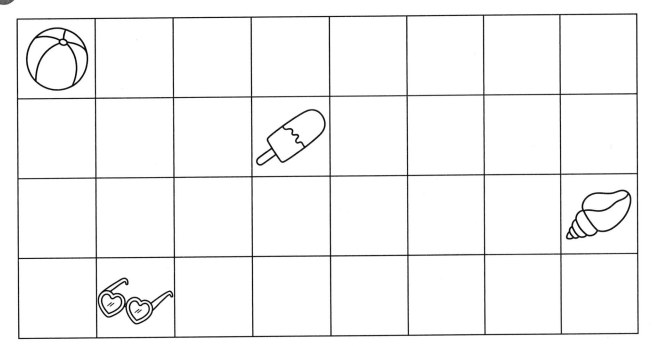

a Draw a ◯ 4 spaces right and 3 spaces down from the 🏐 .

b Draw a △ 2 spaces left and 1 space up from the 🐚 .

I Can Checklist:
Measurement

 Choose and use non-standard units appropriately to measure lengths, and describe the inverse relationship between the size of a unit and the number of units needed. For example,

- *I can* use paperclips to measure the length of my pencil and understand that the shorter the paperclip, the more I will need to cover the length of the pencil.

- *I can* measure the length of my desk using my hand as a non-standard unit, and understand that if I used a smaller hand, I would need more of that unit to measure the desk.

- *I can* explain that if I use bigger blocks to measure the length of my toy car, I would need fewer blocks than if I used smaller blocks.

 Explain the relationship between centimetres and metres as units of length, and use benchmarks for these units to estimate lengths. For example,

- *I can* explain that 100 centimetres make up 1 metre.

- *I can* estimate the length of my bookshelf in metres, then check my estimate using a measuring tape.

- *I can* use the width of my hand as a benchmark to estimate the length of an object in centimetres.

 Measure and draw lengths in centimetres and metres, using a measuring tool, and recognize the impact of starting at points other than zero. For example,

- *I can* use a ruler to measure and draw a line that is 10 centimetres long.

- *I can* measure the length of my room in metres using a tape measure.

- *I can* explain why it's important to start at the zero point when measuring the length of an object.

Measuring Using Non-Standard Units

1 Count the blocks to measure the objects.

a

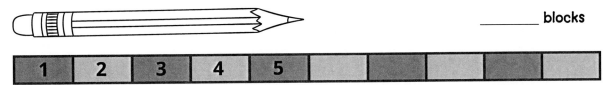

_____ blocks

| 1 | 2 | 3 | 4 | 5 | | | | | |

b

_____ blocks

c

_____ blocks

2 Draw a line that is **9 blocks** long.

Estimate and Measure
Using Non-Standard Units

Estimate and measure length, height, and distance using non-standard units, such as paper clips, shoes, or crayons. Record your measures.

I am measuring the...	I am measuring with...	My estimate	My measurement
length of a...			
height of a...			
distance from...			

I can estimate using non-standard units.

Exploring Units of Length

We use these units to measure **length** or **distance**.

Centimetre (cm)
One centimetre is about the width of a fingernail.

Metre (m)
One metre is about the height of a doorknob.

We measure small things with centimetres.

We measure big things with metres.

Circle the best unit to measure the length of each object.

1

centimetres   metres

2

centimetres   metres

3

centimetres   metres

4

centimetres   metres

5

centimetres   metres

6

centimetres   metres

Measuring Using Centimetres

1 Measure the shape. Write the length in the box.

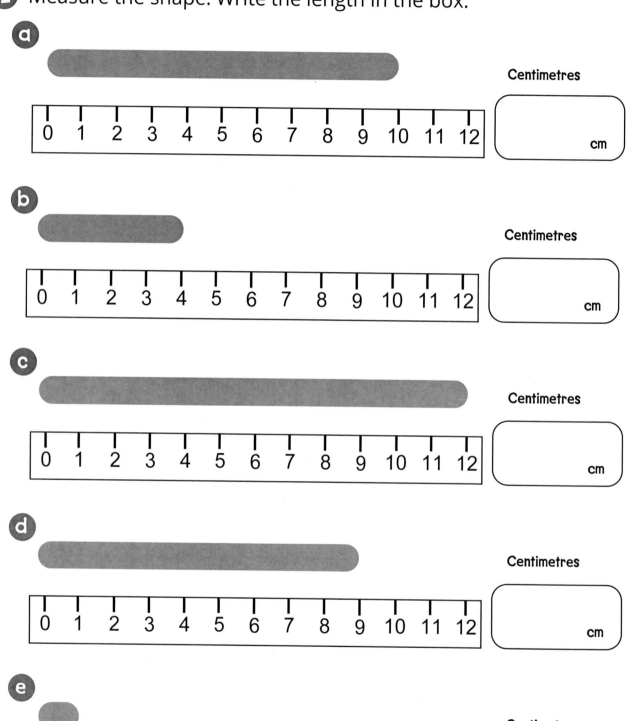

a

Centimetres

cm

b

Centimetres

cm

c

Centimetres

cm

d

Centimetres

cm

e

Centimetres

cm

I can measure using centimetres.

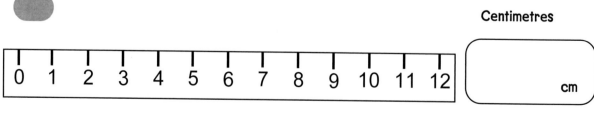

Measuring Using Centimetres (continued)

2 Draw a line that is 6 centimetres long.

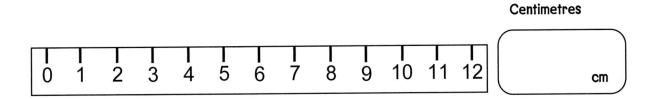

Centimetres

_____ cm

3 Draw a line that is 2 centimetres long.

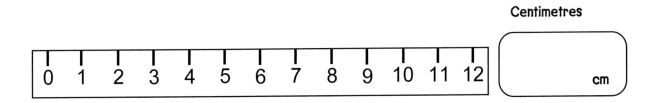

Centimetres

_____ cm

4 Draw a line that is 11 centimetres long.

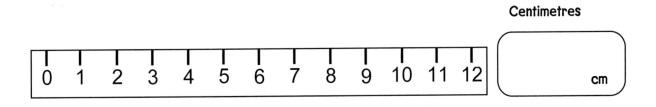

Centimetres

_____ cm

5 Draw a line that is 7 centimetres long.

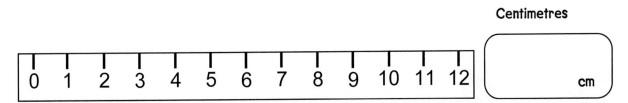

Centimetres

_____ cm

Exploring Perimeter

The **perimeter** is the total distance around a figure.

We can use a unit grid to find the perimeter of any figure.

Each square is 1 unit by 1 unit.

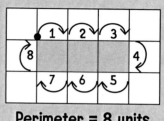

Perimeter = 8 units

1 Find the perimeter of the figure.

a

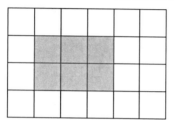

P = _____ units

b

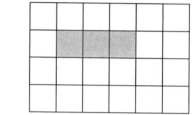

P = _____ units

c

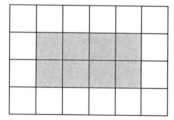

P = _____ units

d

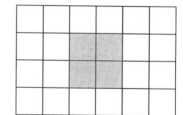

P = _____ units

e

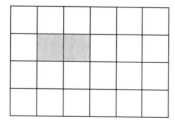

P = _____ units

f

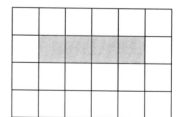

P = _____ units

I can understand perimeter.

Exploring Perimeter (continued)

To find the **perimeter** (distance around),
add the lengths of each side of the shape.

5 + 3 + 5 + 3 = 16 units

The perimeter is **16 units**.

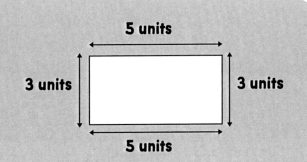

2 Write the side lengths. Add to find the perimeter.

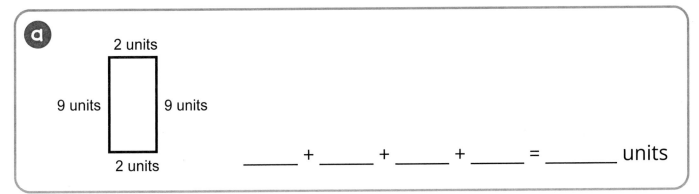

a

2 units

9 units   9 units

2 units

_____ + _____ + _____ + _____ = _____ units

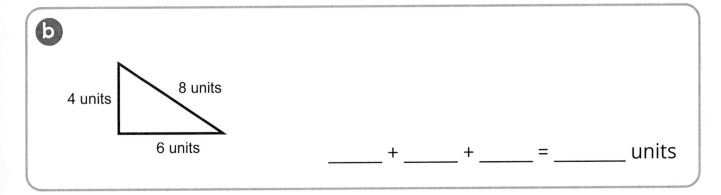

b

4 units   8 units

6 units

_____ + _____ + _____ = _____ units

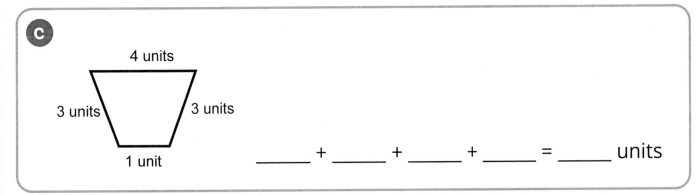

c

4 units

3 units   3 units

1 unit

_____ + _____ + _____ + _____ = _____ units

Exploring Area

Area is the number of units that cover a figure.

[ ] 1 square = 1 unit

Count the number of shaded square units.

The area of the shaded figure is 9 units.

1 Count the number of shaded squares to find the area.

a

_____ square units

b

_____ square units

c

_____ square units

d

_____ square units

I can understand area.

Exploring Area (continued)

2 Draw as many shapes as you can with an area of 8 units squared.

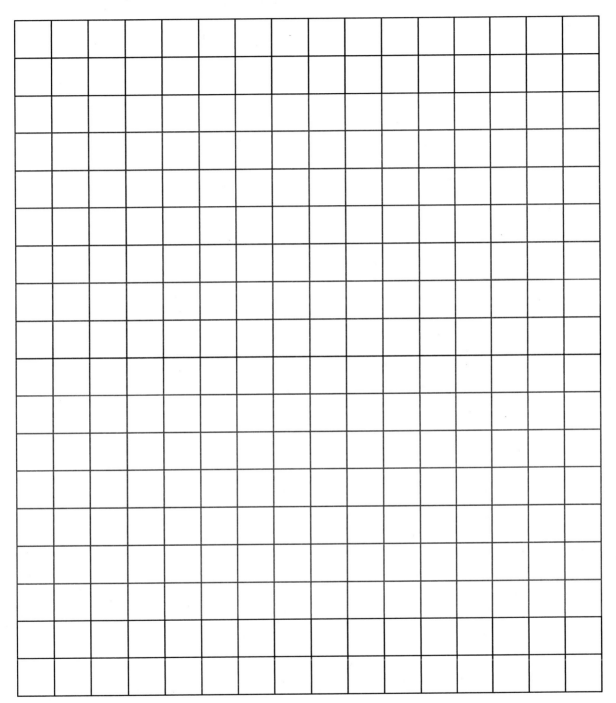

3 Is it possible for two shapes to have the same area but look different? Circle **YES** or **NO**.

YES   **NO**

Exploring Mass and Capacity

Mass measures how much something weighs.

1 Circle and colour the object that has a **greater mass**.

a

b
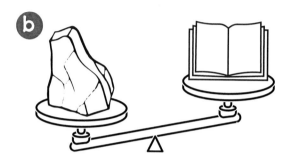

c

d

Capacity is the amount that something can hold.

2 Circle and colour the container that **holds the most**.

I can understand mass and capacity.

Exploring Measurement Tools

Draw a line from the activity to the measurement tool you would use.

You want to know the date. •

You want to measure the length of your book. •

You want to weigh some apples. •

You want to know the temperature. •

You want to know what time it is. •

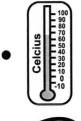

You need to measure a cup of flour to make bread. •

Exploring Temperature

Temperature is a measure of exactly how hot or cold something is. A thermometer is used to measure temperature. Temperature is measured in degrees on the **Celsius** scale.

This thermometer shows **10 degrees Celsius** or **10°C**.

1 Circle the correct temperature.

a

What temperature is it most likely to be in the middle of summer?

–25°C   **25°C**

b

What temperature is it most likely to be in the middle of winter?

–15°C   **15°C**

c

What temperature is it most likely to be while raining in the spring?

–10°C   **10°C**

I can understand temerature.

Exploring Temperature (continued)

2 Use red to colour the thermometer to the given temperature.

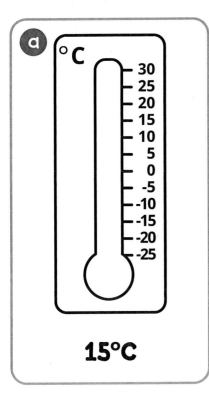

15°C

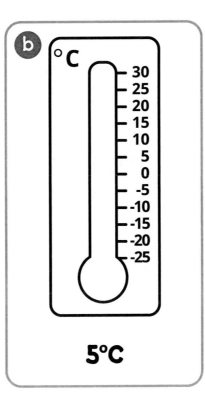

5°C

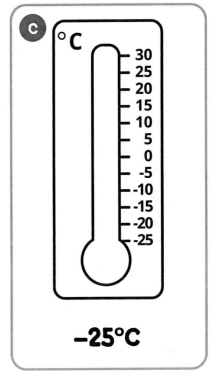

−25°C

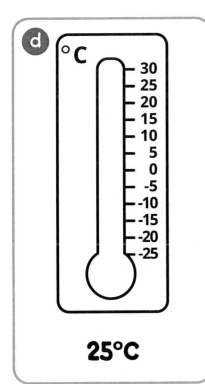

25°C

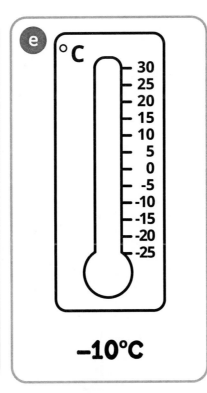

−10°C

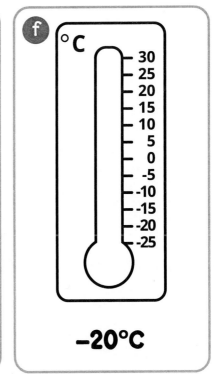

−20°C

Show What You Know!

1 Circle the best unit to measure the length of each object.

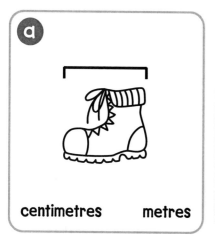

centimetres   metres

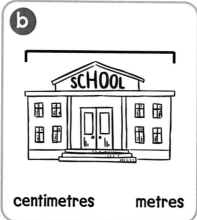

centimetres   metres

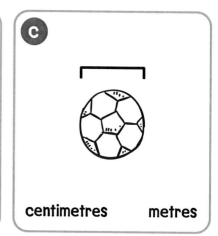

centimetres   metres

2 Draw a line that is 8 centimetres long.

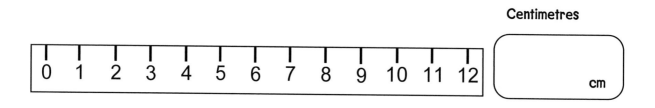

Centimetres

cm

3 Find the perimeter of the figure.

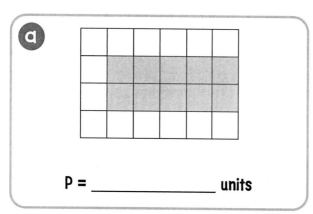

P = _____ units

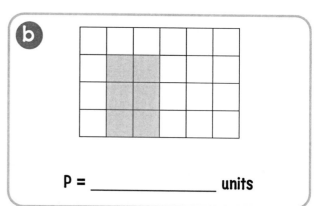

P = _____ units

Show What You Know! (continued)

4 Draw a figure with the given area.

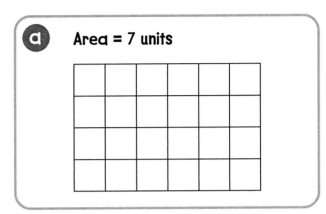

a Area = 7 units

b Area = 10 units

5 Circle and colour the container that **holds more**.

6 Circle and colour the object that has a **greater mass**.

a

b

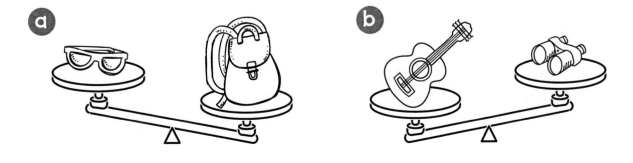

I Can Checklist:
Time

Use units of time, including seconds, minutes, hours, and non-standard units, to describe the duration of various events. For example,

- ***I can*** *use the unit 'minutes' to describe the duration of my favourite cartoon show.*
- ***I can*** *use the unit 'seconds' to describe how long I can hold my breath.*
- ***I can*** *use the unit 'hours' to describe the duration of a school day.*
- ***I can*** *use non-standard units like 'bedtime stories' to describe how long it takes for me to go to bed after dinner.*

Parent Tips:

Make It Fun:
Turn learning into a game! Use flashcards or board games that involve time and dates. There are also plenty of educational apps available that make learning time and dates fun and interactive.

Use a Real Clock:
While digital clocks are everywhere, it's best to start with an analog clock when teaching time. The visual representation of the hands on the clock makes the concept of time more tangible.

Daily Time Checks:
Ask your child what time it is at various points throughout the day. This can help them get used to the idea of time passing.

Complete a Watch Face

Write the numbers on the watch. Draw the minute hand to 12. Draw the hour hand to 4.

Telling Time to the Hour

A clock has an hour hand.
The hour hand is short. It shows the hour.

You can write the time in two ways.
It is **5 o'clock** or **5:00**.

1 Draw a line between the times that are the same.

4 o'clock •   • 2:00

12:00 •   • 4:00

2 o'clock •   • 7 o'clock

7:00 •   • 12 o'clock

2 Write the time in two ways.

a

_____ o'clock or

_____:00

b

_____ o'clock or

_____:00

I can tell time to the hour.   © Chalkboard Publishing Inc

Telling Time to the Hour (continued)

3 Tell the time to the hour. Highlight the hour hand in blue.

a

_____ o'clock

b

_____ o'clock

c

_____ o'clock

d

_____ o'clock

e

_____ o'clock

f

_____ o'clock

Telling Time to the Half Hour

A clock has an hour hand.
The hour hand is short.
It shows the hour.

It is **3 o'clock** or **3:00**.
There are 60 minutes
in an hour.

A clock has a minute hand.
The minute hand is long. It shows
the minutes after the hour.

Count by 5s.
It is 30 minutes after 3 o'clock.
It is **half past 3** or **3:30**.

1 What time is it? Write the time in words.

a

b
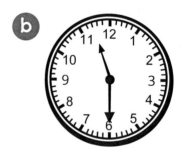

_____   _____

2 What time is it? Write the time in numbers.

a

b

_____   _____

I can tell time to the half hour.

Telling Time to the Half Hour (continued)

3 Tell the time to the half hour. Highlight the hour hand in blue. Highlight the minute hand in red.

half past _____

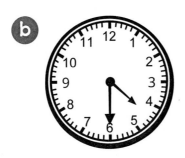

half past _____

half past _____

half past _____

half past _____

half past _____

half past _____

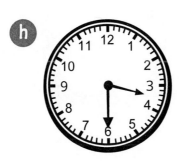

half past _____

half past _____

Telling Time to Quarter Past the Hour

The minute hand points to 3.
The hour hand is just after 8.

It is **quarter past 8** or **8:15**.

Write the time two ways. Highlight the hour hand in blue.
Highlight the minute hand in red.

1

quarter past _____

_____ : _____

2

quarter past _____

_____ : _____

3

quarter past _____

_____ : _____

4

quarter past _____

_____ : _____

5

quarter past _____

_____ : _____

6

quarter past _____

_____ : _____

I can tell time to quarter past the hour. © Chalkboard Publishing Inc

Telling Time to Quarter to the Hour

The minute hand points to 9.
The hour hand is after 7 and close to 8.

It is **quarter to 8** or **7:45**.

Write the time two ways. Highlight the hour hand in blue.
Highlight the minute hand in red.

1

quarter to _____

_____ : _____

2

quarter to _____

_____ : _____

3

quarter to _____

_____ : _____

4

quarter to _____

_____ : _____

5

quarter to _____

_____ : _____

6

quarter to _____

_____ : _____

Months of the Year

List the months of the year in the correct order.

August	1 _____
January	2 _____
May	3 _____
September	4 _____
June	5 _____
February	6 _____
July	7 _____
October	8 _____
March	9 _____
November	10 _____
April	11 _____
December	12 _____

I can write the months of the year.

Reading a Calendar

November						
Sunday	**Monday**	**Tuesday**	**Wednesday**	**Thursday**	**Friday**	**Saturday**
	1 Music	2	3 Gym	4	5	6
7	8 Music	9 Pizza Day	10 Gym	11	12	13
14	15 Music	16	17 Gym	18	19 Field Trip	20
21	22 Music	23 School Fair	24 Gym	25	26	27
28	29 Music	30				

1 Name the month for this calendar.

2 What day of the week is the first day of the month?

3 What day of the week is the last day of the month?

4 What is the date of the field trip?

Show What You Know!

1 Write the time in two ways.

a

_____ o'clock or

_____:00

b

_____ o'clock or

_____:00

2 What time is it? Write the time in words.

a

_____

b

_____

3 Write the time.

a

_____ : _____

b

_____ : _____

c

_____ : _____

Show What You Know! (continued)

4 Write the time.

a

_____ : _____

b

_____ : _____

c

_____ : _____

d

_____ : _____

e

_____ : _____

f

_____ : _____

5 Write the correct month.

a The 8th month of the year: _____

b The 4th month of the year: _____

c The 12th month of the year: _____

Congratulations!

Great Work!

I Did It !

Answers

Representing Numbers in Different Ways p. 6

1. First and third groups **2.** First and second groups

3. Second and third groups **4.** Second and third groups

Counting Tens and Ones p. 7

1. 1 hundred, 3 tens, 3 ones 100 + 30 + 3 133 blocks

2. 6 tens, 4 ones 60 + 4 64 blocks

3. 1 hundreds 1 tens 2 ones 100 + 10 + 2 112 blocks

4. 8 tens 6 ones 80 + 6 86 blocks

Writing Numbers in Written Form p. 8

1. a) seventy b) fifteen c) one hundred eighty-three

   d) one hundred twenty

2. thirty-three **3.** one hundred ninety-four

Writing Numbers in Different Ways p. 9

1. a) 90 + 6 b) 100 + 60 + 4 c) 100 + 10 + 3 d) 100 + 50 + 2

2. a) 138 b) 116 c) 179 d) 124

3. a) 4 tens b) 1 hundred c) 6 ones d) 5 tens

Skip Counting p. 10

1. 25, 30, 35, 40, 45 **2.** 70, 90, 110

3. 90, 100, 110, 120, 130, 140, 150, 160, 170

4. 60, 80, 100, 120, 140, 160, 180

Counting Practice p. 11

1. 160, 170, 180, 190, 200 **2.** 50, 75, 100, 125, 150

3. 158, 160, 162, 164, 166 **4.** 181, 180, 179, 178, 177

5. 90, 80, 70, 60, 50 **6.** 118, 116, 114, 112, 110

Comparing Numbers p. 12

1. < **2.** > **3.** = **4.** < **5.** = **6.** > **7.** > **8.** <

Ordering Numbers p. 13

1. a) 87 b) 165 c) 52 d) 198 **2.** a) 50 b) 100 c) 17 d) 20

3. a) 25, 55, 72, 99 b) 48, 120, 190, 200

4. a) 96, 77, 46, 13 b) 188, 179, 125, 102

5. 41, 33, 24, 17

Identifying Odd and Even Numbers p. 14

Vertical columns of numbers:

Odd, blue: 87, 33, 97, 25, 29, 93, 71, 39, 115, 61, 199, 99

Even, red: 62, 100, 200, 14, 46, 16, 58, 54, 88, 46, 10, 70, 2, 6

Estimating and Counting p. 15

Estimations will vary. **1.** 17 **2.** 33 **3.** 25

Composing Numbers p. 16

1. 163 **2.** 28 **3.** 52 **4.** 195 **5.** 116 **6.** 79

Decomposing Numbers p. 17

1. 100, 4 **2.** 100, 50 **3.** 70, 1 **4.** 100, 30 **5.** 100, 40, 9 **6.** 80, 3

Show What You Know! pp. 18–19

1. a) one hundred forty-five b) 100 + 40 + 5

2. 110, 115, 120, 125, 130 **3.** a) < b) = c) >

4. 89, 125, 167, 180 **5.** 200, 110, 101, 100 **6.** a) 9 tens b) 1 hundred

7. Even **8.** First and second groups **9.** 22 **10.** a) 94 b) 100, 60, 5

Equal and Not Equal Parts p. 21

Ensure shapes are correctly coloured.

Exploring Fractions p. 22

1. a) N-2 D-3 b) N-4 D-6 c) N-1 D-2 d) N-3 D-4

2. a) 4/6 b) 2/4 c) 1/3 **3.** a) 3 b) 2 c) 6 d) 4

Exploring Sets p. 23

1. 1/3 **2.** 3/6 or 1/2 **3.** 1/2

Exploring Halves p. 24

1. a) 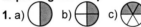 **2.** a) 3 boots b) 5 clocks

Exploring Fourths p. 25

1. a)  **2.** a) 1 ball b) 2 shells

Exploring Thirds p. 26

1. a) b) 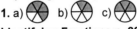 **2.** a) 1 shell b) 2 ice creams

Exploring Sixths p. 27

1. a) b) c)   **2.** a) 1 guitar b) 2 fires

Identifying Fractions p. 28

1. a) 1/3 b) 1/2 c) 1/4

2. a) 1/4 b) 2/3 c) 4/6 d) 2/3 e) 1/2 f) 1/5 g) 3/4 h) 5/6 i) 3/4

Colour the Fractions p. 29

1.   **2.**   **3.**   **4.**   **5.** 6.

7. 3 circles orange **8.** 1 star yellow

Exploring Fraction Bars pp. 30–31

1. Ensure fraction bars are coloured correctly.

2. a) one whole b) 1/3 c) one half d) 1/2

3. b) 1/4 c) 2/3 d) 1/2 **4.** a) b)

Exploring Equal Amounts pp. 32–33

1. No **2.** Yes **3.** No **4.** No **5.** Yes **6.** No

Fraction Word Problems p. 34

1. a) 3/4 **2.** 1/2 **3.** 2/3

Fair Sharing p. 35

1. No **2.** Yes **3.** No

Exploring Fair Shares p. 36

1. 2 each, no **2.** 5 each, no **3.** 1 each, yes, 2 left **4.** 2 each, yes, 2 left **5.** 2 each, yes, 2 left **6.** 4 each, yes, 1 left

Fair Share Word Problems pp. 37–39

1. 2 whole pies each, the remainder can be split in half.

2. a) 2 whole pizzas each, the remainder can be split in thirds

   b) 1 whole cake each, the remainder can be split in fourths

3. a) Yes b) Yes

Show What You Know! pp. 40–41

1. Shapes 1, 4, and 5 **2.** **3.** a) 2/8 b) 1/4

4. a) 1 each, yes, 3 left b) 3 each, no

5. a) 2 squares orange b) 2 stars blue

6. 2 cookies each, there are 2 cookies left over

Answers

7. a) one half   b) 1/4

Doubles Strategy for Addition p. 44

1. 8   **2.** 2   **3.** 12   **4.** 18   **5.** 4   **6.** 14   **7.** 16   **8.** 6   **9.** 10   **10.** 20

Doubles Plus 1 Strategy for Addition p. 45

1. 3   **2.** 17   **3.** 13   **4.** 9   **5.** 7   **6.** 19   **7.** 5   **8.** 15   **9.** 11   **10.** 21

Draw a Picture Strategy for Addition p. 46

1. 10   **2.** 14   **3.** 11   **4.** 14

Exploring Estimation p. 47

1. a) 10 + 10 = 20 b) 30 + 10 = 40 c) 20 − 10 = 10

d) 30 − 10 = 20 e) 10 + 40 = 50 f) 20 + 30 = 50

2. a) less than 50 b) more than 20 c) more than 70

Adding Tens and Ones pp. 48–49

1. a) 10 + 10 + 10 + 1   b) 10 + 1 + 1 + 1 + 1

2. a) 50 + 6 b) 70 + 9 c) 90 + 5 d) 30 + 8

3. a) 45 b) 28 c) 57 d) 62 e) 8, 80 f) 9, 90 g) 8, 80 h) 7, 70

4. a) 77 b) 78 c) 69 d) 37 e) 97 f) 77 g) 58 h) 99

Find the Missing Number p. 50

1. 5   **2.** 3   **3.** 2   **4.** 7   **5.** 7   **6.** 3   **7.** 12   **8.** 4   **9.** 13   **10.** 3

11. 5   **12.** 4   **13.** 7   **14.** 14   **15.** 7   **16.** 7

Addition Riddle p. 51

A) 19 C) 13 D) 6 E) 16 H) 17 I) 12 K) 18 L) 6 N) 14 O) 9

P) 10 R) 20 S) 11 T) 8 U) 5 V) 15 W) 7 X) 11 Y) 4 Z) 9

To prove he wasn't chicken!

Two-Digit Addition Without Regrouping pp. 52–53

1. a) 86 b) 87 c) 79 d) 57 e) 58 f) 95 g) 67 h) 69   **2.** 95

3. A) 66 B) 48 D) 61 E) 67 G) 85 H) 52 I) 77 L) 76 M) 88

N) 79 O) 63 P) 73 Q) 80 R) 97 S) 99 T) 33 U) 50 V) 57

W) 54 Z) 75

With an asteroid belt!

Two-Digit Addition With Regrouping pp. 54–55

1. a) 93 b) 76 c) 62 d) 70 e) 90 f) 65 g) 72 h) 91   **2.** 84

3. A) 42 B) 62 C) 50 D) 46 E) 36 G) 60 H) 75 I) 81 J) 61

K) 94 L) 57 M) 78 N) 63 O) 73 P) 84 R) 80 S) 55 T) 51

U) 91 V) 70 W) 92 X) 95 Y) 90 Z) 71

It had no atmosphere!

Mental Math Strategies for Subtraction p. 57

1. 5   **2.** 6   **3.** 13   **4.** 12

Draw a Picture Strategy for Subtraction p. 58

1. 2   **2.** 7   **3.** 4   **4.** 2

Doubles Strategy for Subtraction p. 59

1. 7   **2.** 3   **3.** 6   **4.** 4   **5.** 5   **6.** 1   **7.** 8   **8.** 10   **9.** 2   **10.** 9

Number Line Strategy for Subtraction p. 60

1. 6   **2.** 3   **3.** 6   **4.** 1   **5.** 4   **6.** 2   **7.** 1   **8.** 5   **9.** 1   **10.** 2

Checking Subtraction by Using Addition p. 61

1. 24   **2.** 25   **3.** 34   **4.** 15   **5.** 15   **6.** 45

Find the Missing Number p. 62

1. 6   **2.** 18   **3.** 11   **4.** 6   **5.** 12   **6.** 9   **7.** 2   **8.** 13   **9.** 9   **10.** 19

11. 8   **12.** 15   **13.** 18   **14.** 12   **15.** 6   **16.** 19

Subtraction Riddle p. 63

A) 20 B) 8 C) 17 D) 7 E) 18 F) 5 G) 6 H) 16 i I 19 J) 9

K) 13 L) 4 N) 12 O) 2 P) 11 R) 1 T) 15 U) 3 W) 10 Y) 14

A bird that will talk your ear off!

Two-Digit Subtraction Without Regrouping pp. 64–65

1. a) 13 b) 24 c) 32 d) 12 e) 54 f) 67 g) 32 h) 12   **2.** 35

3. A) 25 B) 41 C) 30 D) 44 E) 43 H) 31 I) 21 L) 33 M) 20

P) 14 R) 11 S) 32 T) 50 U) 42 Y) 10

Build a sty scraper!

Two-Digit Subtraction With Regrouping pp. 66–67

1. a) 29 b) 38 c) 37 d) 38 e) 28 f) 37 g) 18 h) 78   **2.** 13

3. A) 29 B) 38 C) 9 D) 8 E) 17 F) 79 G) 68 H) 46 I) 36

K) 69 N) 13 O) 37 R) 27 S) 19 T) 34 U) 18 V) 47 Y) 49

Frogs because they croak every night!

Number Fact Families pp. 68–69

1. a) 7 + 9 = 16, 9 + 7 = 16, 16 − 9 = 7, 16 − 7 = 9

b) 5 + 8 = 13, 8 + 5 = 13, 13 − 5 = 8, 13 − 8 = 5

2. a) 8 + 4 = 12, 4 + 8 = 12, 12 − 4 = 8, 12 − 8 = 4

b) 9 + 10 = 19, 10 + 9 = 19, 19 − 10 = 9, 19 − 9 = 10

Addition and Subtraction Problems pp. 70–71

1. a) add, 59 cards b) subtract, 18 more yellow buttons

2. a) add, 81 flowers b) subtract, 31 more apples

Introducing Multiplication p. 72

1. 10, 10   **2.** 8, 8   **3.** 16, 16   **4.** 12, 12

Multiplying Groups p. 73

1. 3 groups of 3, 3 × 3 = 9   **2.** 2 groups of 6, 2 × 6 = 12

3. 4 groups of 2, 4 × 2 = 8   **4.** 5 groups of 4, 5 × 4 = 20

Introducing Division p. 74

1. a) 2 groups of 8, 16 ÷ 8 = 2   **2.** 4 groups of 4, 16 ÷ 4 = 4

3. 3 groups of 2, 6 ÷ 2 = 3   **4.** 2 groups of 5, 10 ÷ 5 = 2

Practising Division p. 75

1. 7   **2.** 3   **3.** 2   **4.** 3   **5.** 3

Multiplication & Division Word Problems pp. 76–77

1. a) multiply, 10 cupcakes b) divide, 2 crayons

2. a) divide, 7 cookies b) multiply, 12 oranges

Patterns in Everyday Life p. 79

1. a) ✹ ☾ ✹ 🍁 b) ☀ ☾   **2.** Answers will vary.

Identifying Patterns on the Hundred Chart p. 80

1. Ensure students correctly colour each number.

2. Every other column is coloured.

3. The 5 and 10s columns are coloured

4. Only the last column is coloured

Answers

Exploring Patterns p. 81

1. a)  b) **B C A** c) **5 6 7**

2. a) 10, 11, 12, 13, 14 b) 100, 120, 140, 160, 180

Translating Patterns pp. 82–83

1. a) ABABAB b)

   c) clap, smack, smack, clap d) ABCDABCD

2. Answers will vary. Examples: a) ○ □ □ ◇, clap, smack,

   smack, quack b) AABB, clap, clap, quack, quack c) ABB,

   clap, quack, quack d) ABBA, clap, quack, quack, clap

Extending Patterns p. 84

1. a) △ ■ b) **12** c) ☆ ☆ d) **56** e) ○ ♡ f) ■ △

   g) **88**

Naming Patterns p. 85

1. ABCABCAB, ABC pattern   2. ABBABBAB, ABB pattern

3. ABCDABCD, ABCD pattern

Growing Number Patterns p. 86

1. a) 10, 12, 14, 16, 18, 20, 22 b) 25, 35, 45, 55, 65, 75, 85

   c) Answers will vary.

2. Answers will vary.

Growing Geometric Patterns p. 87

1. a)  2. Answers will vary.

Shrinking Number Patterns p. 88

1. a) 28, 26, 24, 22, 20, 18, 16 b) 50, 45, 40, 35, 30, 25, 20

   c) Answers will vary.   2. Answers will vary.

Shrinking Geometric Patterns p. 89

1. a)  2. Answers will vary.

Identifying Pattern Changes pp. 90–91

1. a) position, colour b) shape, colour c) shape, colour

   d) position, size

2. a) position b) position, colour c) shape, colour d) shape

   e) position

Creating Patterns pp. 92–93

Answers will vary. Ensure students make patterns matching the

instructions.

Show What You Know! pp. 94–95

1. a) ○ ▦ ▦ b) **2 2 3 3** 2. a) **100** **10** b) ● □

3. a) shape, AAB 4. Example: (R)(G)(B)(Y) 5. AABBAABB

6. a) 30, 35, 40, 45, 50, 55, 60 b) 102, 104, 106, 108, 110, 112, 114

7. a) 140, 130, 120, 110, 100, 90, 80 b) 75, 70, 65, 60, 55, 50, 45

Introducing Variables p. 97

1. a) 7 b) 3 c) 10 d) 3 e) 7 f) 9   2. a) $5 + n = 15$ b) $n - 8 = 4$

Exploring Variables pp. 98–99

1. a) n b) p c) r d) n e) y f) p

2. a) $15 - n = 12$ b) $n + 10 = 25$

3. a) 17 b) 7 c) 6 d) 18 e) 5 f) 28

4. a) 10 b) 1 c) 26 d) 21 e) 11 f) 6

Exploring Addition Sentences p. 100

1. Examples: a) 4 + 4, 2 + 6, 7 + 1 b) 2 + 2, 1 + 3, 3 + 1

   c) 9 + 1, 5 + 5, 7 + 3 d) 4 + 2, 3 + 3, 5 + 1

Balance It p. 101

2. 2   3. 4   4. 5   5. 6   6. 3

Making Equal Addition Expressions p. 102

1. a) = b) ≠ c) ≠

2. Answers will vary. Examples: a) 4 + 4 b) 8 + 1 c) 10 + 5

Finding the Missing Number - Addition p. 103

1. 8   2. 7   3. 6   4. 3   5. 5

Exploring Subtraction Sentences p. 104

Answers will vary. Examples: 1. 4, 1; 3, 2; 2, 3   2. 5, 4; 4, 5; 8, 1

3. 3, 3; 4, 2; 2, 4

4. 8, 2; 9, 1; 5, 5

Balance It p. 105

2. 3   3. 2   4. 1   5. 5   6. 4

Making Equal Subtraction Expressions p. 106

1. a) ≠ b) = c) ≠

2. Answers will vary. Examples: a) 4 – 1 b) 10 – 4 c) 5 – 3

Finding the Missing Number - Subtraction p. 107

1. 1   2. 5   3. 4   4. 3   5. 3

Show What You Know! pp. 108–109

1. a) 8 b) 8 c) 12   2. a) 16 b) 5 c) 5 d) 20

3. Answers will vary. Examples: a) 4 + 4, 6 + 2 b) 3, 2; 4, 1

4. a) 4 b) 5   5. ≠   6. 7 – 3   7. 11

Coding in Everyday Life! p. 111

1. Coloured items: car, controller, video game

2. Answers will vary.

Reading Code p. 112

1. 👓 2. 🍦

Writing Code pp. 113–114

1. a) →→→↓↓ b) →↓↓↓ c) ↑↑↑→

2. Answers will vary. Examples:

   1→→→→↓2   2↑↑→→→3   3↓↓↓↓←4   4←←←←↑5

Concurrent Code p. 115

Answers may vary. Examples: 1. 6   2. 7   3. Pig

Altering Code pp. 116–117

1. a) Beach b) →→↓←←   2. ↑←←←↑

3. Answers will vary. Examples: a) ↑→→→ b) →→↓ c) →→→↓↓→

Show What You Know! pp. 118–119

1. 🎨 2. →→→↓↓ 3. Mouse gets there in fewer steps.

4. ↑→→→→

Answers

Getting to Know Coins p. 121

Counting Coins p. 124

1. Top set **2.** Bottom set **3.** Top set **4.** Top set **5.** Bottom set
6. Top set

Show Two Different Ways to Make the Same Amount p. 125

Answers will vary. Examples: **1.** 2 dimes; 1 dime, 2 nickels

2. 3 quarters; 2 quarters, 2 dimes, 1 nickel **3.** 1 loonie, 3
quarters, 1 dime; 1 loonie, 2 quarters, 3 dimes, 1 nickel

Counting Canadian Bills p. 126

1. a) $50 b) $105 c) $100 d) $112

Comparing Money Amounts p. 127

1. a) $80 < $100 b) $200 > $60 c) $30 < $120

Showing Bill Amounts in Different Ways p. 128

Answers will vary. Examples: **1.** 2 twenties, 1 ten; 1 twenty, 3 tens
2. 2 fifties; 1 fifty, 2 twenties, 1 ten **3.** 1 twenty, 1 five; 2 tens, 1
five **4.** 2 hundreds; 1 hundred, 2 fifties

Buying Sports Equipment p. 129

1. $55 **2.** $125 **3.** Answers will vary.

Show What You Know! pp. 130–131

1. a) Top set b) Bottom set

2. Answers will vary. Examples: a) 2 quarters, 1 dime; 1 quarter, 3
dimes, 1 nickel b) 1 quarter, 2 dimes; 1 quarter, 1 dime, 2 nickels

3. $50 < $55 **4.** a) $26 b) $84 c) $15

Exploring Venn Diagrams p. 134

Tammy, Anna, Penny

Sorting into a Venn Diagram p. 135

1. Even: 16, 32, 44 Above 50: 97, 105, 81 Both: 58, 60

Sorting into a Carroll Diagram pp. 136–137

1. Summer tops: Tank top, T-shirt Summer bottoms: shorts

Winter tops: Parka, sweater, sweatshirt

Winter bottoms: pants, snow pants

2. Household pet on land: cat, dog

Household pet underwater: fish

Not household pet on land: squirrel, lion, cow

Not household pet underwater: sea turtle, sea jelly

Exploring Tally Charts pp. 138–139

1. yellow: 10 blue: 5 purple: 3 a) yellow b) purple c) 15

2. dog: 9 cat: 8 bird: 4 a) dog b) bird c) 17 d) 4

Exploring Pictographs pp. 140–141

1. a) hockey b) football c) 8 **2.** a) 5 b) Bailey c) Anita d) 5

Exploring Bar Graphs pp. 142–143

1. a) Yo-yos b) hula hoops c) 4 **2.** a) snowy b) 12 c) 4

Exploring Line Plots pp. 144–145

1. a) 4 b) 3 c) 1 and 4

2. 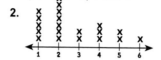 a) 2 b) 2 c) 4

Finding the Mode pp. 146–147

1. a) 10 b) 8 **2.** a) 5 b) 100 c) 4 d) 3 e) 20 f) 1

Representing Data in Different Ways pp. 148–149

1. Dog: |||| Cat: |||| ||| Hamster: | Bird: ||||

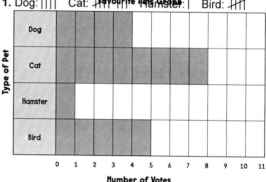

2. a) cat b) hamster c) 9 d) 7 e) 1

Show What You Know! pp. 150–151

1. Soccer: |||| | Hockey: |||| |||| Basketball: |||
Baseball: ||||

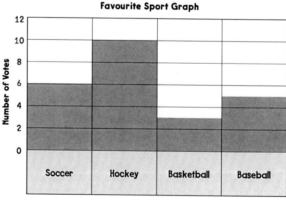

2. a) 2 b) 8 **3.** a) 50 b) 4

Exploring Probability p. 153

1. possible **2.** impossible **3.** certain **4.** possible

What Is the Probability? pp. 154–155

1. a) likely b) impossible c) unlikely d) certain

Answers

2. and 3. Answers will vary.

Thinking About Likelihood pp. 156–157

1. a) unlikely   b) likely   c) likely   d) unlikely

2. pepperoni: 10   cheese: 9   mushrooms: 3   onions: 3

   a) 3   b) Answers will vary.

Show What You Know! pp. 158–159

1. a) certain   b) impossible   **2.** a) unlikely   b) unlikely

3. Answers will vary.   **4.** a) 8   b) likely

Identifying 2D Shapes p. 161

Ensure shapes are correctly coloured.

Exploring Polygons p. 162

Triangle: 3 sides, 3 vertices   Square: 4 sides, 4 vertices

Pentagon: 5 sides, 5 vertices   Hexagon: 6 sides, 6 vertices

Octagon: 8 sides, 8 vertices

Geometry and Spatial Sense p. 163

1. square, triangle, trapezoid   **2.** triangle   **3.** pentagon, hexagon

4. all shapes

Exploring Symmetry p. 164

1. yes   **2.** yes   **3.** no   **4.** yes   **5.** no   **6.** no

Decomposing Shapes p. 165

1. two triangles   **2.** two half-circles   **3.** triangle and trapezoid

4. three triangles

3D Figures p. 166

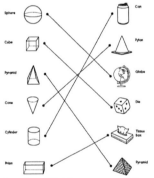

Sorting 3D Figures p. 167

1. sphere, cylinder, cone   **2.** cube, pyramid, prism

3. sphere, pyramid, cone   **4.** a) pyramid   b) cube

Congruent Shapes p. 168

1. blue   **2.** blue   **3.** green   **4.** green   **5.** blue   **6.** blue

Positional Words p. 169

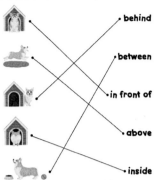

Reading a Map p. 170

1. 15   **2.** 3   **3.** restaurant   **4.** house   **5.** museum

Location and Movement p. 171

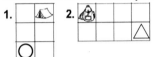

3. 2 spaces left and 3 spaces down

4. 3 spaces right and 2 spaces up

Show What You Know! pp. 172–173

1. Ensure the correct shapes are coloured.   **2.** a) yes   b) no   c) no

3. a) blue   b) green

4.

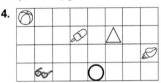

Measuring Using Non-Standard Units p. 175

1. a) 5 blocks   b) 1 block   c) 3 blocks

2.

Estimate and Measure Using Non-Standard Units p. 176

1. Answers will vary.

Exploring Units of Length p. 177

1. metres   **2.** centimetres   **3.** metres   **4.** centimetres

5. centimetres   **6.** metres

Measuring Using Centimetres pp. 178–179

1. a) 10 cm   b) 4 cm   c) 12 cm   d) 9 cm   e) 1 cm

2. `0 1 2 3 4 5 6 7 8 9 10 11 12`   **3.** `0 1 2 3 4 5 6 7 8 9 10 11 12`

4. `0 1 2 3 4 5 6 7 8 9 10 11 12`   **5.** `0 1 2 3 4 5 6 7 8 9 10 11 12`

Exploring Perimeter pp. 180–181

1. a) 10   b) 8   c) 12   d) 8   e) 6   f) 10

2. a) 2 + 9 + 2 + 9 = 22 units   b) 4 + 8 + 6 = 18 units

   c) 4 + 3 + 1 + 3 = 11 units

Exploring Area pp. 182–183

1. a) 8   b) 6   c) 13   d) 12   **2.** Answers will vary. a) Yes

Exploring Mass and Capacity p. 184

1. a) 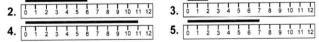 b)   c)   d)   **2.**

Answers

Exploring Measurement Tools p. 185

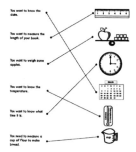

Exploring Temperature pp. 186–187

1. a) 25°C   b) –15°C   c) 10°C

2. a)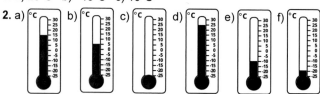

Show What You Know! pp. 188–189

1. a) centimetres   b) metres   c) centimetres

2.    **3.** a) 14   b) 10

4. Answers will vary.

5.   **6.** a) 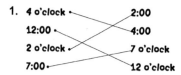   b)

Complete a Watch Face p. 191

Telling Time to the Hour pp. 192–193

1.
4 o'clock ⟶ 4:00
12:00 ⟶ 7 o'clock
2 o'clock ⟶ 2:00
7:00 ⟶ 12 o'clock

2. a) 8 o'clock, 8:00   b) 5 o'clock, 5:00

3. a) 4   b) 10   c) 9   d) 5   e) 6   f) 7

Telling Time to the Half Hour pp. 194–195

1. a) 9 o'clock   b) half past 11   **2.** a) 2:30   b) 1:00

3. a) 10   b) 4   c) 12   d) 9   e) 6   f) 1   g) 5   h) 3   i) 8

Telling Time to Quarter Past the Hour p. 196

1. quarter past 12, 12:15   **2.** quarter past 9, 9:15   **3.** quarter
past 6, 6:15   **4.** quarter past 2, 2:15   **5.** quarter past 4, 4:15

6. quarter past 7, 7:15

Telling Time to Quarter to the Hour p. 197

1. quarter to 10, 9:45   **2.** quarter to 1, 12:45   **3.** quarter to 6, 5:45

4. quarter to 8, 7:45   **5.** quarter to 2, 1:45   **6.** quarter to 7, 6:45

Months of the Year p. 198

1. January   **2.** February   **3.** March   **4.** April   **5.** May   **6.** June

7. July   **8.** August   **9.** September   **10.** October   **11.** November

12. December

Reading a Calendar p. 199

1. November   **2.** Monday   **3.** Tuesday   **4.** November 19

Show What You Know! pp. 200–201

1. a) 10   b) 6   **2.** a) half past 12   b) half past 6

3. a) 12:45   b) 7:45   c) 9:15

4. a) 8:30   b) 6:00   c) 6:15   d) 12:30   e) 2:15   f) 5:00

5. a) August   b) April   c) December